Penguin Masterstudies
Advisory Editors:
Stephen Coote and Bryan Loughrey

Drama:
Text into Performance

Peter Reynolds

Penguin Books

Penguin Books Ltd, Harmondsworth, Middlesex, England
Viking Penguin Inc., 40 West 23rd Street, New York, New York 10010, U.S.A.
Penguin Books Australia Ltd, Ringwood, Victoria, Australia
Penguin Books Canada Ltd, 2801 John Street, Markham, Ontario, Canada L3R 1B4
Penguin Books (N.Z.) Ltd, 182–190 Wairau Road, Auckland 10, New Zealand

First published 1986

Made and printed in Great Britain by
Richard Clay (The Chaucer Press) Ltd, Bungay, Suffolk
Filmset in 9/11pt Monophoto Times by
Northumberland Press Ltd, Gateshead, Tyne and Wear

'Weigel's Props' by Bertholt Brecht and translated by John Willett from
Poems 1913–1956 is reprinted by permission of Methuen, London.

Penguin Masterstudies

Drama: Text into Performance

Peter Reynolds was born in Cromer, Norfolk, in 1946. After leaving school he received professional theatre training at the Central School of Speech and Drama, and at the London Academy of Music and Dramatic Art. He subsequently worked in the theatre in Britain and the United States before going to Sussex University to read English. He is now a lecturer in drama at the Roehampton Institute, and lives in Lewes, Sussex.

For Kim

Contents

Acknowledgements

I should like to thank Bryan Loughrey for having the nerve to ask me to write this book, and for keeping it whilst I completed it. I am also grateful to Stuart Cosgrove, Cicely Berry, and students, colleagues and friends at the Roehampton Institute, in particular Neil Taylor and Susanne Greenhalgh. My greatest debt is to my wife, to whom this book is gratefully and lovingly dedicated.

... one thing afflicts me, to think that scenes invented merely to be spoken should be enforcively published to be read ...

John Marston's preface to *The Malcontent*, 1604.

Introduction

When you walk into a bookshop, or even into your local library, you usually have to look quite hard to find the shelf, or portion of a shelf, that holds the selection of plays. Novels, on the other hand, seem to be everywhere – even the local supermarket will offer a selection, albeit generally of a sensational or lurid nature. Hardly anybody, it seems, wants to buy or read plays of whatever kind. Were it not for their presence on the GCE syllabus and the reading lists of humanities degree courses, most would probably never be printed. By contrast, there is in this country a tolerably healthy market for those who wish to sell performances of plays in the theatre. It appears that an *audience* for plays exists, but not much of a *readership*. It is highly unlikely that this book will have such a dramatic effect that supermarket managers across the country will rush out and fill their shelves with new and old plays for customers suddenly hungry to read them, but I do hope that those of you who read it will come to regard the reading of plays as potentially an exciting and enjoyable experience. After all, give a group of students of dramatic literature the task of performing a play before an audience and they will leap to it with alacrity. I want to tap some of that enthusiasm and direct it towards what I call 'active' reading.

It is impossible to pick up a copy of a play and read it without on some level recreating the events it relates in the theatre of the mind's eye. This is a natural and instinctive response, but perhaps because it is natural and instinctive, it tends to be taken for granted and, in any case, is not easily subjected to analysis. This book aims to enrich the reading of plays by encouraging the reader to be both more aware, and more informed, about the judgements and decisions being taken (often unconsciously) when dramatic literature is transformed imaginatively into a theatrical event. In order to develop this awareness, it is necessary to look at how a play is made in rehearsal and in performance, and by whom. We need to acknowledge that the text performed in a theatre before an audience is the result of a collaborative effort on behalf of author, actors, designer, director and audience. The reading of a play ought to mirror the excitement of that collaboration and, above all, to accept as necessary and legitimate the need to take interpretative decisions which require evaluative risks. The reader of plays must also take on board the idea that the printed text of a dramatist is incomplete and partial without the dimension of performance, be it imagined or practically realized.

Of course this is not a new idea. Over the last decade there has been a tremendous growth in critical literature acknowledging that plays need to be studied in the context of performance. Many new insights and enhanced understanding have been developed as a consequence. This book is a practical proponent of the same basic premise: that an alliance of the intellect and the creative imagination is necessary to bring a text to life. You have to *make it happen*. You must employ your intellectual skills to open up ideas in the printed text that seem significant to you, and then take delight in using your imagination to animate them.

This is not a book intended as a guide on how to produce plays, but one which seeks to make the reader aware that a dramatist's printed text is *a* text, not *the* text. It is the starting point, and serves as a blueprint for necessary further action. Actors, directors, designers and audiences all make their own texts from what is given them by the dramatist, but what they make is *not* the same thing as what has been printed, although the printed text is where the process of interpretation usually starts.

'Active' reading of a play demands that the reader take decisions. First he or she must recognize, and then organize, the huge variety of visual and aural signs that consciously and subliminally are at work making an imaginary performance text in the theatre of the mind's eye. He or she must accept that no single sign, or generator of that sign, be it the gesture of an actor at a particular moment, or a colour used significantly in a designer's setting, is *the* text, but that any performance text is a blend of many different signs and signals. Every collective expression of those signs and signals comprises the play in performance, and each is different from the previous one. Indeed, every witness of a performance sees their own text and not that of their neighbour. That this is so becomes evident from even the most cursory glance at dramatic criticism, let alone from the greatly contrasting discussions of what actually took place, and its significance, that results whenever a lively group of people watch purportedly the same performance of a play. Just as all the participants in a performance text, and all the members of its audience, have to make their own text, so you, the reader, have to make *your* text, and that text will be the result of the synthesis you choose to create after juggling with the different but complementary textual statements that comprise the transition from text into performance.

Perhaps I ought to explain why William Shakespeare is the dramatist most often referred to in this book – it is, after all, called *Text Into Performance*, not *Shakespeare's Text Into Performance*. There were a number of factors which resulted in this decision. The first was pragmatic. I assume that most readers will have read at least one or two of his plays and, with any luck, will also have seen performances of them in the theatre, on television and on film. The second, and more important, consideration for the focus on Shakespeare was simply an acknowledgement of the fact that his work is performed in the British theatre today with greater frequency, and arouses more interest, than that of almost any other dramatist, living or dead. Because of this powerful and sustained influence on theatre practice, an exploration of how Shakespeare organized his ideas into a form which he confidently expected to be effective in perform- ance may teach us much about how dramatists think in general. Giving in-depth consideration to one of the dramatists discussed also makes it possible to examine how the theatrical product of performance, so eagerly yet often so unknowingly consumed, is actually made.

In addition to plays by Shakespeare (notably *Hamlet*, *Richard III* and *Richard II*), the book also examines the stagecraft of the nineteenth and twentieth centuries, and in particular, that of Ibsen (*A Doll's House* and *Hedda Gabler*); Chekhov (*Three Sisters* and *The Cherry Orchard*); and Pinter (*The Caretaker*) and Edward Bond (*Saved*).

1 The Printed Text

Whether it is in the classroom or in the rehearsal-room, work towards a text-into-performance must begin with very close scrutiny of the dramatist's text as it has been printed and published. As this is the beginning of this book and of our scrutiny of dramatic texts, it is as well to emphasize the importance of reading and re-reading that text *before* any collective decisions are made and the rehearsal debate begun. Whatever creative ideas may subsequently emerge as the result of your debate with yourself or others over what you come to see as the texts of actor, director and designer, you must be able to argue for their authority from the basis of a sound knowledge of the starting point for all subsequent textual statements: the dramatist's text. Your task is to get to know a text and to develop enough confidence to enable you to begin to release some of its latent potential for dramatic expression through the exercise of your *informed* imagination. It is not necessary to design, direct, or act in plays (although some of you may well do so) but you should begin to be able to translate what is given on the printed page into an imaginative, and effective, theatrical event.

What follows in this chapter, and indeed in the rest of the book, is not a complete and exhaustive study of the complexities of making an imaginary performance text out of a printed one. What I shall concentrate on is what I have found useful and interesting in my own study of text-into-performance, and what I feel is too often neglected when the emphasis on the study of plays is literary as opposed to dramatic.

Textual Authority

A performance of a play is an ephemeral thing, changing from day-to-day and all too soon forgotten. A play committed to print, however, seems at once altogether more permanent and to carry with it an aura of authority. But that authority, seen as a basis for interpretation, is not always what it seems. This is particularly true in the case of plays by Shakespeare and his contemporaries. When you begin to study their work, remember that *no* manuscript of Shakespeare's plays survives. Indeed, there are very few manuscripts available to scholars or anyone else of plays of the Elizabethan and Jacobean period. In a sense, the part of this chapter that deals with Shakespeare could more accurately be entitled the

'Editor's Text', for, the modern edition of the play that you are likely to read and study, and indeed the edition used as a basis for making modern texts into performances in our theatre, has been put together by editors from early (sixteenth and seventeenth century) printed versions of the plays, published in small editions after the play itself had ceased to be performed regularly. In these quarto or folio editions, the division of the text into acts and scenes, the punctuation and spelling, and the stage directions, are all largely the work of the first compositors who set the type from a manuscript probably supplied by the theatre. Indeed, some of these early printed versions do not indicate any act or scene divisions, and these have been added later by subsequent editors.

Shakespeare and other dramatists of the period, seem to have taken very little obvious interest in the publication of their work, largely, I think, for economic rather than artistic reasons. Shakespeare was a member, a shareholder in fact, of a theatrical company which made its profits from performances, not from selling the rights to publication. There was, in any case, no real protection of copyright for dramatists, and in order to prevent other groups of actors from stealing successful theatrical material, plays were only published after their immediate audience had been exhausted, and even the actors themselves were given only a copy of their own parts (their roles) lest the temptation to sell the whole to the highest bidder proved too much for them. Therefore we should remember that our modern printed text is, in a very real sense, only an approximation of what Shakespeare himself may, or may not, have written. What was set in type by the first printers of Shakespeare's work no doubt reflects closely what was written, and perhaps more closely than that, what was performed on the stage, but its authority is not absolute.

In the practice of Shakespeare's *theatre*, the authority of the written text was secondary to that of the spoken, and what was considered to be theatrically effective, that is what made people actually want to pay money to visit the theatre, was the paramount consideration of both actors and dramatist. This was a commercial theatre for which Shakespeare and his contemporaries produced, as it were, working drawings – blueprints on which to base performances that could and would be adapted by the players as circumstances (meaning audiences) required.

When these Comedies and Tragedies were presented on the stage, the actors omitted some scenes and passages (with the Author's consent) as occasion led them; and when private friends desired a copy, they then (and justly too) transcribed what they acted. (From the Stationers Address (1647) to the collected plays of Beaumont and Fletcher.)

That does not mean to say that a dramatist such as Shakespeare was always happy with what was done on the stage to his material, for, as Hamlet remarks to the players who visit Elsinore:

... let those that play your clowns speak no more than is set down for them. For there be of them that will themselves laugh to set on some quantity of barren spectators to laugh too, though in the mean time some necessary question of the play be then to be considered. That's villainous, and shows a most pitiful ambition in the fool that uses it.

(III, ii, lines 37–43)

What it does mean is that the modern printed edition of a Shakespearean play is not the absolute authority as to what should be permitted in the making of a performance text. Its authority, although considerable, is ultimately speculative and editorial rather than demonstrably authorial. This is important, and we do need to be reminded of it, if only because of the authority that the printed word currently commands in our culture.

Stage Directions

The closer we come to our own time, the greater the authority of the printed text becomes. Editions of modern plays are now often published simultaneously with their first performance. Certainly playwrights today write to be read and to be seen. They can exercise total control over what is printed, even if they cannot control, as much as they would like, what is actually performed. The awareness of modern dramatists of the needs of the reader, and their desire to influence the production of their work in the theatre, leads to detailed instructions in the printed text as to how the performance text should be staged. These stage directions carry the unmistakable authority of their author and it would be foolish and perverse to disregard them entirely. But in the text that we have of a Shakespeare play, or indeed that of almost any other pre-nineteenth-century dramatist, the stage directions do *not* carry the same prescriptive weight. When you begin to analyse Shakespeare's printed text, treat the stage directions with caution, as a guide rather than a rule as to how to 'read' a scene. Remember that Shakespeare tailor-made his text to fit a small group of professional players whose work and ability he knew and understood. The group was small in number compared to today's large national companies, not through any natural reluctance of the general populace to thrust themselves upon the stage as performers, but because those who earned their living through what was an entirely commercial enterprise, knew that the fewer they were in number the greater the share of the proceeds of their art each could expect to receive. Therefore, with a permanent company of players totalling some ten to twelve full-time professionals, the doubling and trebling of roles for most actors was a requirement of their employment: the cast list for *Hamlet* for instance, lists no less than thirty-three named roles in addition to attendants, guards, sailors and so on. Of course many of the smaller roles, particularly those not required to speak, would have been played by the so-called 'hired men', the Elizabethan equivalent of today's film extras. But all the main roles would have been covered by the men of the permanent company, thus the two actors who open *Hamlet* as Barnardo and Francisco are equally likely to have ended it as Osrick and Fortinbras, having played First Player and Ophelia in between. When you see printed at the head of the page of your modern edition the list of characters who are to appear in the following scene, remember that the absence of a particular character may originally have been for *practical* (the actor was required for another role) rather than interpretative reasons. Thus in Act I, Scene ii of *Hamlet* the directions state:

Flourish.
Enter Claudius, King of Denmark, Gertrude the Queen, and the Council, including Polonius with his son Laertes, Hamlet, Voltemand, Cornelius, and attendants

But is the list complete? I suggest that it is quite legitimate for you, the active reader, to suggest and argue for the presence in this scene of Ophelia. After all, her father and brother are both present. Of course she is given no words to speak but, as we will see later, silent characters are often amongst the most visually eloquent of those on stage. My point is simply that Shakespeare's stage directions are not sacrosanct; you must judge for yourself their appropriateness and not let the circumstances of the original playing conditions limit unnecessarily your freedom to re-interpret your text-into-performance. The only absolutely reliable stage directions in Shakespeare are those that come from the text spoken by the actors themselves. If a character says, as Barnardo does in the first scene of *Hamlet*,

BARNARDO: Sit down awhile,
        And let us once again assail your ears,
        That are so fortified against our story,
        What we have two nights seen.
                (lines 30–33)

and to which the reply is

HORATIO: Well, sit we down,
        And let us hear Barnardo speak of this.
                (line 34)

17

It is quite obvious what should happen, and you would have to *adapt* the text, as opposed to interpreting it, if you wanted to see things any differently. But rarely are things quite so clear cut.

When you begin to study the plays of the nineteenth and twentieth centuries, the stage directions have more authority. Those in a printed edition of a play by Ibsen, Chekhov or Shaw for example, bear the unmistakable stamp of the author. Those dramatists, unlike Shakespeare and his contemporaries, took care to control the production of the printed text, and what they suggest in terms of stage directions as to how the theatre language of the performance text should be staged, are clearly what they hoped to see enacted, either literally or imaginatively. For this reason alone, a study of stage directions of this period is informative. None the less, they should still be regarded by you, the active reader, as a guide and not a rule. As the actress Janet Suzman remarked

... all stage directions are a drag. If they are good ones, they describe to you the author's intentions as regards the characters' inner state. If they are bad, they dictate to you and should be disregarded.[1]

But the closer we come to contemporary dramatic writing, the more care and attention we must none the less give to stage directions. Many modern dramatists have consciously realized, and indeed rediscovered, the expressive potential in a theatre language composed not only of words, but also and equally, of physical gesture, grouping and visual metaphor. This non-verbal text is articulated for the reader through detailed stage directions, and you cannot begin to understand how the performance text is designed to work unless you study them carefully. You cannot, for example, begin to come to terms with some of the great plays of our century, such as Beckett's *Waiting for Godot*, without giving equal recognition to what Beckett says the characters *do*, as to what he says they do, and do not, *say*.

A good example of stage directions that clearly indicate how a contemporary dramatist's text uses expressive non-verbal language is seen in Harold Pinter's opening directions for *The Caretaker*:

MICK is alone in the room, sitting on the bed.
He wears a leather jacket.
Silence.
He slowly looks about the room looking at each object in turn. He looks up at the ceiling, and stares at the bucket. Ceasing, he sits quite still, expressionless, looking out front.
Silence for thirty seconds.

A door bangs. Muffled voices are heard.
MICK turns his head. He stands, moves silently to the door, goes out, and closes the door quietly.
Silence.
Voices are heard again. They draw nearer, and stop.
The door opens. ASTON and DAVIES enter, ASTON first, DAVIES following, shambling, breathing heavily.
ASTON wears an old tweed overcoat, and under it a thin shabby dark-blue pinstripe suit, single-breasted, with a pullover and faded shirt and tie. DAVIES wears a worn brown overcoat, shapeless trousers, a waistcoat, vest, no shirt, and sandals. ASTON puts the key in his pocket and closes the door. DAVIES looks about the room.

The temptation for the reader is often to pass over such detailed directions in the mistaken impression that the play begins with the opening lines of dialogue. Let us look at them closely and try to re-create what an audience might see if this text were faithfully articulated in performance. They first spy a lone figure sitting in an extraordinary room, filled, it seems, with objects that bear very little relationship to each other. The objects themselves are familiar and recognizable, but the arrangement of them is not. The man alone in the room does nothing; there is silence and stillness on the stage. The audience watch and listen, expecting imminent 'action'. By looking at every object in the room in turn, the actor escorts the eye of the audience on a tour of his surroundings. Thirty seconds of silence is a *long* time in the theatre, particularly so at the beginning of a performance – time it for yourself and see. Try looking at television and note the amount of action covered in that time.

The silence at the beginning of *The Caretaker* produces tension in the audience, tension finally broken by the noise of a door off-stage banging. Then there are more noises produced by muffled voices. This performance text is posing a number of questions to the audience by flouting their expectations of what usually happens at the beginning of a play (remember that *The Caretaker* was first performed in 1960). What *is* happening? The audience have been watching the stage for at least two-to-three minutes, and nothing has been 'said'. All the signs are confusing. Has an actor forgotten his cue? The puzzlement of the audience seems about to be lifted by the apparently imminent arrival of the owners of the muffled voices, but they are denied the satisfaction of an entrance, and given instead the exit of the one character they could at least see. His exit is very deliberately spelled out by Pinter. There are five distinct movements for the actor to follow; the head turns, he stands, he moves to the door, goes out, closes it. All this takes time and seems purposeful, yet what the purpose might be is anything but clear. More silence follows, with a now completely empty stage. The actor's move looked deliberate, as if he knew what he was doing, yet nothing can be seen to have resulted from it. Has he gone off to find out for himself what is happening? Will a representative of the management appear at any moment and apologize, explaining that there has been an unfortunate accident back-stage and the performance cannot continue? But nothing happens, and no one appears. Then, at last, the sound of approaching voices. But they stop! Then at last the door opens to reveal, not the actor who exited through it a few minutes earlier, but two new actors. They do not speak immediately but wait before at last beginning to speak the opening lines of the spoken text. But there has been perhaps four or five minutes of playing time in which, if we read the stage directions carefully, we can see a complicated and skilful stagecraft at work, creating a performance text that inspires tremendous feelings of curiosity, tension, and even frustration in the audience who experiences it. The text generates suspense by continually challenging the audience to make sense of what happens when familiar objects and events are rendered unfamiliar, and therefore interesting, by a carefully controlled series of apparently random actions. If you, the reader, can grasp the significance of these stage directions, and not pass over them in your rush to reach the spoken word, you will see for yourself what Kenneth Tynan referred to in his review of the play's first performance as

Mr Pinter's bizarre use (some would call it abuse) of dramatic technique, his skill in evoking atmosphere . . .[2]

This, Tynan was quick to acknowledge, is 'what holds one theatrically'.

Indeed, what holds an audience theatrically is clearly the essential ingredient in dramatic writing. In constructing a play designed for performance, a playwright recognizes the essential importance of the opening five to ten minutes of playing time. The audience brings with it a collective goodwill towards what is about to happen: they *want* to listen, watch, and enjoy. That goodwill must be built upon and not dissipated, for once it is lost it is unlikely to be won back. A performance text must reach out for, hold, and sustain the attention of an audience. We have just seen something of how a modern dramatist makes the means to achieving this clear through his stage directions. Because of the detail supplied by Harold Pinter, the task for the active reader of *The Caretaker* is relatively straightforward. A lot of the imaginative work has already been done; all he or she needs to do is to recognize the dramatic significance of the information made available. However, in Shakespeare, the dramatist's text leaves the active reader with a good deal more work to do if he is to make a performance text out of a printed one.

Recognizing the importance of how a play begins, and that Shakespeare does not spell out to reader, actor, director, designer or anyone else exactly how his text should be made into a performance, I want to look in some detail at the beginning of one of his most famous plays. The opening stage directions in *Hamlet* are minimal, but if we work patiently through the modern printed text we will begin to see that there are clues within it as to possible presentational strategies. What we will certainly see is the number and nature of the interpretative decisions – indeed the risks – that need to be taken in order for you, as an active reader, to make a unique, imaginative, theatrical event out of a piece of probably very familiar dramatic literature.

Do read the opening scene before you go on, otherwise what follows below will not mean anything to you. Remember that what I am offering you is *my* imaginary creation of this text-into-performance. It has no particular merit or status, and is certainly not *the* text. It becomes *a* text by drawing upon a range of textual statements that I find significant. Adopt its method, its way of working, but do not necessarily adopt its conclusions.

    Enter Francisco and Barnardo, two sentinels   I.1
BARNARDO: Who's there?
FRANCISCO: Nay, answer me. Stand and unfold yourself.
BARNARDO: Long live the King!
FRANCISCO: Barnardo?
BARNARDO: He.
FRANCISCO:
  You come most carefully upon your hour.
BARNARDO:
  'Tis now struck twelve. Get thee to bed, Francisco.
FRANCISCO:
  For this relief much thanks. 'Tis bitter cold,
  And I am sick at heart.
BARNARDO:
  Have you had quiet guard?   10
FRANCISCO: Not a mouse stirring.
BARNARDO:
  Well, good night.
  If you do meet Horatio and Marcellus,
  The rivals of my watch, bid them make haste.
    Enter Horatio and Marcellus
FRANCISCO:

I think I hear them. Stand ho! Who is there?

HORATIO:

  Friends to this ground.

MARCELLUS: And liegemen to the Dane.

FRANCISCO:

  Give you good night.

MARCELLUS: O, farewell, honest soldier.

  Who hath relieved you?

FRANCISCO: Barnardo hath my place.

  Give you good night.   *Exit*

MARCELLUS: Holla, Barnardo!

BARNARDO: Say –

  What, is Horatio there?

HORATIO: A piece of him.

BARNARDO:

  Welcome, Horatio. Welcome, good Marcellus.   20

HORATIO:

  What, has this thing appeared again tonight?

BARNARDO:

  I have seen nothing.

MARCELLUS:

  Horatio says 'tis but our fantasy,

  And will not let belief take hold of him

  Touching this dreaded sight twice seen of us.

  Therefore I have entreated him along

  With us to watch the minutes of this night,

  That, if again this apparition come,

  He may approve our eyes and speak to it.

HORATIO:

  Tush, tush, 'twill not appear.

BARNARDO: Sit down awhile,   30

  And let us once again assail your ears,

  That are so fortified against our story,

  What we have two nights seen.

HORATIO: Well, sit we down,

  And let us hear Barnardo speak of this.

BARNARDO:

  Last night of all,

  When yond same star that's westward from the pole

  Had made his course t'illume that part of heaven

  Where now it burns, Marcellus and myself,

  The bell then beating one –

    Enter the Ghost

MARCELLUS:

  Peace, break thee off. Look where it comes again.   40

BARNARDO:
> In the same figure like the King that's dead.

MARCELLUS:
> Thou art a scholar. Speak to it, Horatio.

BARNARDO:
> Looks 'a not like the King? Mark it, Horatio.

HORATIO:
> Most like. It harrows me with fear and wonder.

BARNARDO:
> It would be spoke to.

MARCELLUS: Speak to it, Horatio.

HORATIO:
> What art thou that usurpest this time of night,
> Together with that fair and warlike form
> In which the majesty of buried Denmark
> Did sometimes march? By heaven I charge thee, speak.

MARCELLUS:
> It is offended.

BARNARDO: See, it stalks away.   50

HORATIO:
> Stay. Speak, speak. I charge thee, speak.   *Exit the Ghost*

MARCELLUS:
> 'Tis gone and will not answer.

BARNARDO:
> How now, Horatio? You tremble and look pale.
> Is not this something more than fantasy?
> What think you on't?

HORATIO:
> Before my God, I might not this believe
> Without the sensible and true avouch
> Of mine own eyes.

MARCELLUS: Is it not like the King?

HORATIO:
> As thou art to thyself.
> Such was the very armour he had on   60
> When he the ambitious Norway combated.
> So frowned he once when, in an angry parle,
> He smote the sledded Polacks on the ice.
> 'Tis strange.

MARCELLUS:
> Thus twice before, and jump at this dead hour,
> With martial stalk hath he gone by our watch.

HORATIO:
> In what particular thought to work I know not.
> But, in the gross and scope of mine opinion,

23

This bodes some strange eruption to our state.

MARCELLUS:

Good now, sit down, and tell me he that knows 70
Why this same strict and most observant watch
So nightly toils the subject of the land,
And why such daily cast of brazen cannon
And foreign mart for implements of war,
Why such impress of shipwrights, whose sore task
Does not divide the Sunday from the week.
What might be toward that this sweaty haste
Doth make the night joint-labourer with the day,
Who is't that can inform me?

HORATIO: That can I.
At least the whisper goes so. Our last King, 80
Whose image even but now appeared to us,
Was, as you know, by Fortinbras of Norway,
Thereto pricked on by a most emulate pride,
Dared to the combat; in which our valiant Hamlet –
For so this side of our known world esteemed him –
Did slay this Fortinbras; who, by a sealed compact
Well ratified by law and heraldry,
Did forfeit, with his life, all these his lands
Which he stood seised of, to the conqueror;
Against the which a moiety competent 90
Was gagèd by our King, which had returned
To the inheritance of Fortinbras,
Had he been vanquisher, as, by the same covenant
And carriage of the article designed,
His fell to Hamlet. Now, sir, young Fortinbras,
Of unimprovèd mettle hot and full,
Hath in the skirts of Norway here and there
Sharked up a list of lawless resolutes
For food and diet to some enterprise
That hath a stomach in't; which is no other, 100
As it doth well appear unto our state,
But to recover of us by strong hand
And terms compulsatory those foresaid lands
So by his father lost. And this, I take it,
Is the main motive of our preparations,
The source of this our watch, and the chief head
Of this posthaste and romage in the land.

BARNARDO:

I think it be no other but e'en so.
Well may it sort that this portentous figure
Comes armèd through our watch so like the King 110

That was and is the question of these wars.
HORATIO:
  A mote it is to trouble the mind's eye.
  In the most high and palmy state of Rome,
  A little ere the mightiest Julius fell,
  The graves stood tenantless and the sheeted dead
  Did squeak and gibber in the Roman streets –
  As stars with trains of fire and dews of blood,
  Disasters in the sun; and the moist star
  Upon whose influence Neptune's empire stands
  Was sick almost to Doomsday with eclipse.   120
  And even the like precurse of feared events,
  As harbingers preceding still the fates
  And prologue to the omen coming on,
  Have heaven and earth together demonstrated
  Unto our climatures and countrymen.
     Enter the Ghost
  But soft, behold, lo where it comes again!
  I'll cross it, though it blast me.
     He spreads his arms
  Stay, illusion.
  If thou hast any sound or use of voice,
  Speak to me.   130
  If there be any good thing to be done
  That may to thee do ease and grace to me,
  Speak to me.
  If thou art privy to thy country's fate,
  Which happily foreknowing may avoid,
  O, speak!
  Or if thou hast uphoarded in thy life
  Extorted treasure in the womb of earth,
  For which, they say, you spirits oft walk in death,
  Speak of it.
     The cock crows
        Stay and speak. Stop it, Marcellus.   140
MARCELLUS:
  Shall I strike it with my partisan?
HORATIO:
  Do, if it will not stand.
BARNARDO: 'Tis here.
HORATIO: 'Tis here.

                              Exit the Ghost

MARCELLUS:
  'Tis gone.
  We do it wrong, being so majestical,

> To offer it the show of violence,
> For it is as the air invulnerable,
> And our vain blows malicious mockery.

BARNARDO:
> It was about to speak when the cock crew.

HORATIO:
> And then it started, like a guilty thing
> Upon a fearful summons. I have heard   150
> The cock, that is the trumpet to the morn,
> Doth with his lofty and shrill-sounding throat
> Awake the god of day, and at his warning,
> Whether in sea or fire, in earth or air,
> Th'extravagant and erring spirit hies
> To his confine. And of the truth herein
> This present object made probation.

MARCELLUS:
> It faded on the crowing of the cock.
> Some say that ever 'gainst that season comes
> Wherein our Saviour's birth is celebrated,   160
> This bird of dawning singeth all night long.
> And then, they say, no spirit dare stir abroad;
> The nights are wholesome; then no planets strike;
> No fairy takes; nor witch hath power to charm.
> So hallowed and so gracious is that time.

HORATIO:
> So have I heard and do in part believe it.
> But look, the morn in russet mantle clad
> Walks o'er the dew of yon high eastward hill.
> Break we our watch up. And by my advice
> Let us impart what we have seen tonight   170
> Unto young Hamlet. For, upon my life,
> This spirit, dumb to us, will speak to him.
> Do you consent we shall acquaint him with it,
> As needful in our loves, fitting our duty?

MARCELLUS:
> Let's do't, I pray. And I this morning know
> Where we shall find him most conveniently.   *Exeunt*

Exposition, Mood, Atmosphere and Tension

At the head of the printed page of the modern Penguin edition of this play
the following appears:

Enter Francisco and Barnardo, two sentinels.

You get very little help from such sparse information. There is no geographical location indicator, and although it is just conceivable that in the original performance conditions a member of the cast held up a board with the location written on it, it is unlikely that such a device was employed because it would have slowed the pace of the action if it were repeated every time the location changed. In any case, as we shall see, once the spoken text begins, it is not required. That spoken text is where you will find the necessary information to enable you to set the scene. The opening exchange between Barnardo and Francisco clearly shows that Francisco is on guard, alone, *before* the entrance of Barnardo. Most modern theatres either don't possess, or don't make use of, a stage curtain that can conceal the acting area prior to the beginning of the performance, and the open-air theatre in which *Hamlet* was originally staged certainly didn't have one. The first decision for the reader is therefore, to decide how, and when, to get the actor playing Francisco on to the stage, and what he should do when he gets there. Let us, for the sake of argument, have him on-stage at his post from the minute the first members of the audience enter the auditorium. We have no curtain, and the actor is there for all to see. What then should we want that actor to be doing and showing? What signals is he sending out to the audience? He is on guard. You can discover clues as to how to enact that guard from what is subsequently spoken. The dialogue reveals that it is night, cold, silent and still. Those are the key words that the actor playing Francisco needs to note in order to begin to make the necessary atmosphere and mood of the opening of the play. He also has to convey whether or not his guard is ceremonial, or whether he is there because of a real need for security. Is he therefore relaxed and bored, or tense and alert? Once you have established his dramatic priorities as an actor, you must then decide how long he has to wait before the entrance of Barnardo. We have already seen, in Harold Pinter's text, the potential effectiveness of silence and waiting. Here you have to decide when to break the silence of the watch by the entrance on to the stage of Barnardo, and the utterance of the first *spoken* text of the performance.

The opening verbal exchange between the two actors seems quick and urgent in contrast to the silence that may have preceded it. They speak in short staccato sentences. Ask yourself why the play begins with a question; why does Barnardo need to ask 'Who's there?' Does he not recognize Francisco? In fact, both characters appear to need time to identify the other. This may indicate that in the original performance both actors were to wear costumes that included a helmet with a visor which, when down, covered the face, perhaps to show that this guard is one in which it is necessary to be armed to the teeth. But equally Shakespeare is signalling to the audience that the scene is taking place at night, and the actors take time to see one another because they need to demonstrate to the audience in the open-air theatre in broad daylight, that, on the stage, it is 'dark'. That convention is strengthened and confirmed aurally when they hear Barnardo actually announce the time of day. To make it quite clear, he says not only that it has 'now struck twelve', but that it is time for Francisco to go to bed.

Entrances on to the stage are always significant dramatically. Not only do they introduce a new actor, or give an opportunity for an actor who has been seen previously to re-establish his contact with the audience, but they also change the *shape* and *pace* of the scene by the addition of their physical presence. The entrance of Horatio and Marcellus (like that of Davies and Aston) is preceded by an off-stage noise indicated by Francisco's 'I think I hear them.' This sound may be friendly or hostile but it is evident from Francisco's challenge that he is not prepared to take any chances. We can, I think, assume that he moves towards the entry point of Horatio and Marcellus to make the challenge. The confrontation mirrors that of the play's opening lines, and, again, reinforces the convention of darkness by the twice repeated 'Give you good night.'

The exit of Francisco leaves Barnardo alone with the two newcomers to the scene. Again he appears to have trouble recognizing them. Because they are some distance away (Francisco having halted their entrance upstage), Barnardo needs to ask, in response to Marcellus's cry of greeting 'Say, What! is Horatio there?' His uncertainty is only made certain when Horatio crosses the stage towards him with arm outstretched to offer his hand in greeting: 'A piece of him.'

Shakespeare stages this opening changing of the guard both to establish the time of day and to create an appropriate atmosphere of mystery and tension. He also needs to show that, in this place at this time, there is an atmosphere of secrecy and even conspiracy. Francisco feels that something is wrong, 'I am sick at heart', but he is not made privy to the secret shared between Barnardo, Marcellus and Horatio. When they are alone they begin to reveal what is behind the tension they, and through their enactment, the audience, have experienced. Shakespeare is careful not to give too much away too quickly. Horatio does not ask about a ghost. He asks, far more effectively from the point of view of the audience, about 'this thing'. The audience then learn something very strange has happened *on previous occasions*:

MARCELLUS: What, has this thing appear'd *again* to-night?
(line 21, author's italics)

Slowly the audience are let into the secret, made a part of the conspiracy. When Marcellus speaks in response to Horatio's question, 'this thing' becomes 'this dreaded sight twice seen of us'. At this point for the audience, and indeed for Horatio, the phenomenon could be almost anything: a monster, a devil or a ghost. Whatever it is, the audience are presumably keen to find out more, and, at this point, Horatio acts as the representative of the audience by giving the kind of sceptical response which makes Bernardo tell more. He 'once again' attempts to convince Horatio of the reality of what they have experienced.

The direction given by Shakespeare through Barnardo for the actors to adopt a particular *grouping* on stage is significant. They are to 'sit down' for two reasons. Firstly, because in sitting they are in an attitude of listening to a story – an attitude in which the listeners are relatively relaxed and, literally, off guard. Secondly, the visual memory of the audience in the theatre will later need to recall that soon-to-be-interrupted story-telling, and the act of sitting will be the key that triggers its recall.

As active readers we have to do more than simply note Shakespeare's stage direction, we have to do something as a result. In your (imagined) performance text you have to decide where the actors will sit and how. As you will see, your decision is important. Let us say that the three are placed as far down-stage towards the audience as possible. Barnardo, the story-teller, is slightly up-stage of his listeners, and perhaps squatting on his haunches so that when he begins his tale he can direct what he says out across the actors and into the audience. Look for a moment at what he says: it is in a language appropriate to a ghost story. Again there is the repetition of the convention of darkness: it is night, and the stars are out. The probable striking of the bell by the stagehands serves both to remind the audience of time passing from the ''tis now struck twelve' of line 7 to 1.00 a.m. and the cue to herald the entry of the Ghost. If the positioning of the actors is as suggested above, then the audience (on- and off-stage) will see the appearance before the story-teller. In a near-contemporary performance of Christopher Marlowe's *Doctor Faustus* in Exeter, a riot almost ensued because of the appearance on the stage of too many 'devils'. It is not difficult, therefore, to anticipate a cry which, unfortunately, we only hear at the pantomime, and then from children, of 'Look out! Behind you!!' For however familiar the Elizabethans may have been with the appearance of ghosts on their stages, they were certainly never completely sanguine or blasé about it. As Hamlet himself later remarks:

... The spirit that I have seen
May be a devil, and the devil hath power
T'assume a pleasing shape ...

(II, ii, lines 596–8)

It is left to the actor playing Marcellus to let the audience make the connection between what they can now see, and the 'thing' they have previously heard of:

MARCELLUS: ... Look where it comes *again*!

(I, i, line 40, author's italics)

Barnardo then identifies the Ghost on behalf of the amazed audience as 'In the same figure like the King that's dead.' Horatio's attempts to question the apparition are closely followed by the audience, who are by now as keen to know the answers as he is. But both are denied the satisfaction of an immediate explanation.

An obvious problem with the Ghost's entry into the action comes when you begin to think what it looks like. When Jonathan Pryce played Hamlet a few years ago in a production at London's Royal Court Theatre by Richard Eyre, the Ghost was never actually seen on stage at all (the opening scene was cut entirely), but was represented simply and effectively as a disembodied male voice that seemed to come from within Hamlet himself. Shakespeare's text gives us a clear idea of what *he* wanted to see. Horatio, at line 60, indicates how the Ghost should appear in performance when he refers to it as wearing armour. But however you choose to represent it, what is important textually is that the audience see a man equipped to go to war: a king in military uniform rather than a king in civilian clothes or robes of state. The text also offers a clue as to how the actor playing the Ghost should perform, as Marcellus points out in line 66:

With *martial stalk* hath he gone by our watch.

(author's italics)

The Ghost does not remain on-stage for very long. When it has gone, and the three actors are left alone again, there is a danger of the audience experiencing a dramatic anticlimax. The build-up to the Ghost's entrance created tension and an air of expectancy in the theatre, which is in danger of becoming dissipated. Shakespeare counteracts this by a simple but clever device: he has Marcellus repeat Barnardo's original injunction to 'sit down'. This movement, especially if the grouping is similar to the previous occasion, triggers the visual memory of the audience into recalling that the last time such an appeal was complied with it heralded the Ghost's appearance. As soon as the action is completed, the audience watch and listen, expecting more excitement. But of course they don't immediately get what they expect. After their attention on the speaker is almost guaranteed, Shakespeare uses the focus not for a further episode in a ghost story, but for a very different tale concerning politics and war.

The attention of the audience on what Horatio is saying begins to be rewarded when the tone of his speech changes and signals another shift in the mood and atmosphere of the performance. From line 80 to 107 he has recalled the events in the recent past that have led to the present situation of political confrontation. He speaks like a disinterested observer, using a calm and legalistic language full of references to 'sealed compact(s)', 'inheritance' and things 'Well ratified by law and heraldry'. But between lines 112 and 125 there is a radical change as Horatio moves from contemplation of the dry facts of the world's current political realities to a thrilling story of the historical and mythical past. He uses a highly charged language which links the past to the present and speaks of 'the sheeted dead', of 'blood', 'Disasters' and of 'Doomsday'. It is possible that by having Horatio, the scholar and sceptic, use such theatrical language to describe the events surrounding the fall of Julius Caesar, Shakespeare intended his audience to recall their own theatrical memory of those very events, spoken of and staged in his own play – *Julius Caesar* at the Globe not so very long before *Hamlet*. What the change in Horatio's language certainly does succeed in doing is to alter the atmosphere, and so prepare the audience for the second entry of the Ghost. To put it at its most basic, Shakespeare is trying to scare the audience.

The second entrance into the playing area by the Ghost is as inconclusive as the first. It fails to provide the audience, or indeed Horatio, Barnardo and Marcellus, with the answers they are seeking: why is it there, and what does it want? Indeed the whole scene up to this point has raised the temperature of the action by posing a series of questions and then refusing to answer any of them. Something is most certainly very wrong, but everyone is in the dark as to what it is. The emotions of the audience have been engaged by the performance text, and they have witnessed the beginning of, if not a horror, then certainly a ghost story. But the coming of dawn in the action of the scene also heralds the prospect of some enlightenment in the extraordinary events the audience have witnessed. As Horatio says, when young Hamlet is brought into the action, 'This spirit, dumb to us, will speak to him.' (line 172). What a wonderful preparation for the entry of an actor this scene is. All that has happened has been an exercise in atmospheric preparation for Hamlet's entry: he is the key that will unlock the subsequent action.

In looking at scene one in this kind of detail, we can see how the printed

31

text of a Shakespeare play contains within it guidelines to how the reader can create an imagined performance, full of atmosphere and feeling. If we learn to read the signs, reading can, like the theatre experience itself, be a sensuous as well as a cerebral experience. I want now to continue to look at scene one of *Hamlet*, this time exploring how Shakespeare organizes the events on the stage in order both to capture and then sustain the attention of the audience.

Dramatic Structure: Rhythm and Pace

The opening scene is constructed in a very clever but simple way which varies the shape and pace of the action. The action is divided into three parts: the opening section begins at the moment when the audience collectively focuses on to Francisco on guard, and lasts until the Ghost has made his first exit. What distinguishes this series of actions from subsequent ones is that its pace, once the spoken text comes into play, is uniformly fast. There is an urgency in the initial exchanges between Francisco and Barnardo marked by their exchange of short sentences. This initial pace is sustained by the rapid movements off and on to the stage, and the appearance of the Ghost itself signals a literally frantic rush of movement to discover what it wants.

After the Ghost's exit the second section begins, lasting until the second sighting. This mid-section of the scene is longer than the other two. It is much calmer and more deliberate than the first, containing as it does less action but more spoken language, and a good deal more information. Most of the time, the actors themselves help the reflective mood and slower pace by themselves simply being still, sitting and listening to what is being said. There are no exits or entrances to disturb the stage picture, and the short sentences of the first section are replaced by much longer phrases, and by speakers who speak without interruption for several minutes at a time instead of for a matter of seconds.

The third and final section of the scene begins when the entry of the Ghost shatters the relative calm of the middle section and literally scatters the seated actors across the stage. The pace is speeded up by Horatio's desperate repetition of 'Speak to me', and the attempts to strike at the Ghost indicate fast movements of the players around the stage, each actor moving from a sedentary position to an active, mobile one. After the Ghost has departed, the pace drops slightly, but the end of the scene is on a distinctly up-beat note. Marcellus, Barnardo and Horatio leave the stage with a sense both of urgency and of purpose. They want to get to Hamlet quickly and tell him what has happened for, 'This spirit, dumb to us, will speak to him.' (line 172). The audience are left eagerly awaiting the sequel. It is on Hamlet that their expectations are now focused.

Stage Time

The three-part structure of this scene is also distinguished by the differences in time that each section presents. The action is compressed, then elongated, then compressed again at the end. An audience cannot remain in a heightened state of expectation for very long, and certainly not for a whole play. Therefore, in this scene, and throughout the play as a whole, the moments of high excitement are inevitably followed by periods of relative calm. This movement and variety is reflected in the changes in stage time in the scene (it moves from before midnight to dawn). In section one, stage time changes little, just over one hour in fact, from before midnight to midnight ('tis now struck twelve), through to one o'clock (the ghost last appeared when the bell struck one and presumably does so again). The middle and slower-paced section covers, appropriately enough, a much longer period of stage time. It moves from shortly after one o'clock in the morning to just before the break of dawn; perhaps some four hours. The final section takes us from that time just before dawn, signalled by the crowing of the cock ('the trumpet to the morn'), to Horatio's sighting of dawn itself:

But look, the morn in russet mantle clad
Walks o'er the dew of yon high eastward hill.
                    (lines 167–8)

and finally on to the very last line of the last section where Marcellus establishes that it is now morning

Let's do't, I pray. And I this morning know
Where we shall find him most conveniently.
                    (lines 175–6)

This scene then shows a tremendous compression of time, but it works in performance because of the different paces of the three-part structure.

We have explored how the first scene of *Hamlet* is put together, how it plays on the emotions and the curiosity of the audience, and how Shakespeare balances the focus of the audience between moments of tension and relaxation. Finally I want to look at the whole of the first act in terms of its dramatic organization and structure. Variety for the eye and ear of the audience is, I think, one of the key factors in making Shakespeare such a potentially powerful and exciting force in performance. Let us look for a minute at the shape of the first act in terms of the varying number of actors on-stage at any one time. Scene one uses five. They make eight separate movements either on to or off the playing area. You can break the movement down as follows: lines 1 to 14 use two actors; 15 to 18 use four; in 19 to 39 there are three; in 39 to 51 the number increases again to four; lines 52 to 125, the long mid-section of the scene, have three again, who, on 126 are joined by a fourth; and then from 142 until the close of the scene there are again three actors.

Scene one uses a small number of actors but constantly changes their number on-stage. Scene two (the council chamber), is in very marked contrast to the first. It uses a much larger number of actors, *at least* eleven if you accept that the councillors and attendants total four. The sparsely populated opening scene is replaced by a stage that now seems crowded with actors. There are other notable changes from scene one. The actor who speaks first (playing Claudius) talks without interruption for thirty-nine lines, unlike the opening of the preceding scene where no actor spoke for more than a few lines at one time. But this second scene has, in common with the first, variety in its shape signalled by the changing number of actors on the stage. At line 41 the eleven are reduced to nine on the exit of Voltimand and Cornelius, and then, at line 128 there is a really radical change in the shape of the scene when all the actors leave the stage except Hamlet. Then the audience see for the first time in performance an actor alone. After his soliloquy, the number of actors is changed to four by the entrance of Horatio, Marcellus and Barnardo. They remain together until line 254 when Hamlet is left alone again for the closing four lines of the scene. Thus in Act I, Scene ii the pattern of movement is: eleven actors down to nine; nine down to one; one up to four; and four down again to one.

Scene three begins with the entrance of two actors (Laertes and Ophelia) who, after fifty-two lines, are joined by a third (Polonius). Laertes leaves at line 87 leaving Ophelia and her father to end the scene after a further forty-nine lines. This scene is the simplest so far in terms of its structure and the number of actors used. But the fourth scene of the act is far more complex and mirrors much of the action of the first. It opens with the entry of three actors (Horatio, Hamlet and Marcellus) who, at line 38, are joined by a fourth (the Ghost). At line 86 Hamlet and the Ghost exit, leaving Horatio and Marcellus alone until the end of the scene. The final scene opens with the two actors playing Hamlet and the Ghost entering together. They remain together for ninety-one lines, the most extensive duologue we have yet seen, until the Ghost exits leaving Hamlet alone. At line 112 his solitude is broken first by the sound of voices coming from off-stage, and then, at line 116, by the actual entry of Horatio and Marcellus. At line 149 the voice of the actor playing the Ghost joins in intermittently until line 181. The rest of the scene and the first act is then played out by Hamlet, Horatio and Marcellus; we end the first act as we began the play, with three actors.

There must be literally dozens of exits and entrances of different characters in this opening act: really a tremendous amount of movement is going on – far more so than in most modern plays. Nothing ever stands still for very long. The location too is mobile: it changes from outside (scene one) to inside (scene three) back to outside again (in four and five). What takes place in those changing locations also changes, from events concerning the supernatural (in one, four and five) to the public and ceremonial life at court (scene two) to the private and domestic world shown in the exchange between the Polonius household in scene three.

Juxtaposing

Recognizing how Shakespeare organizes the incidents and events that are put into his dramatist's text is a very important part of trying to understand the way in which meaning is manufactured by performance. The order in which the audience sees the action unfolding is carefully contrived: certain events are scenically juxtaposed in order to make dramatic effects and meaning. The juxtaposing of Act 3 Scenes ii and iii of *Julius Caesar* will illustrate this technique. You will remember that in scene two Mark Antony and Brutus both have an opportunity to address a crowd of plebeians directly following the assassination of their leader, Julius Caesar. Brutus, one of the leaders of the conspiracy to kill Caesar, and one who took part directly in his death, speaks to the crowd in order to explain to them the reasons behind this drastic action. His audience are potentially extremely hostile to him, but his cool rational speech wins their attention. Brutus uses a rhetorical trick to win the sympathy of his audience. He explains his action, and that of his fellow conspirators, as necessary because

Not that I loved Caesar less, but that I loved Rome more.   (III, ii, line 21)

Convinced he is now speaking as their representative his listeners respond positively:

FIRST PLEBEIAN: This Caesar was a tyrant.
THIRD PLEBEIAN: Nay, that's certain.
                    We are blest that Rome is rid of him.   (lines 70–71)

Brutus is, of course, speaking to two audiences, one on-stage and the other in the auditorium. In this scene, as in all others that you read, you must use your imagination to stage the performance text for, without it, the full impact of the scene cannot be gathered. The stage directions state that Brutus enters a pulpit. Whatever this may have been on the Elizabethan stage, it is certain that Shakespeare intends Brutus to have an elevated position. Let us decide to make that position up-stage of the plebeians so that when he addresses them, what he says is also directed out into the body of the auditorium. Both sets of audience not only listen, but each makes decisions as to how they will respond. This same process continues immediately when it is Mark Antony's turn to speak. He too ascends into the pulpit and both on-stage and off-stage audiences are moved, in all likelihood, by the sheer power of Antony's rhetorical skill. He works on the emotions of his listeners and actually descends from the pulpit on to the same level as the crowd and thus associates himself with them. They, and we, are drawn to him. We all of us know or remember

Friends, Romans, countrymen, lend me your ears;   (line 74)

but few of us recall anything of what *Brutus* actually said. What, in performance, had seemed moments before a reasonable position, is transformed into an act of gross treachery, and the crowd on stage turn into an avenging mob:

SECOND PLEBEIAN: Most noble Caesar! We'll revenge his death.
THIRD PLEBEIAN: O royal Caesar!   (lines 244–5)

The actor playing Mark Antony must set out to persuade and move *both* sets of audiences, and if he succeeds, then the juxtaposing of this scene with the one that follows will make sure that the audience in the theatre *feels* the effect, and *sees* the results of what can happen when people are ruled by emotion and not by reason. At the end of scene two, after the mob has rushed off in a rage, Antony reveals to those of his listeners confined to their seats, that he is fully aware of what he has succeeded in doing:

ANTONY: Now let it work. Mischief, thou art afoot,
          Take thou what course thou wilt.   (lines 261–2)

The course of that mischief is now to be made plain. Antony has stirred up violent feelings which the audience will now witness being turned into violent acts. In scene three, Antony's exit is immediately followed by the entrance of the poet, Cinna. He is confronted by the enraged mob who, on discovering that his name happens to be shared by one of the conspirators, attack him there and then in the most violent and obscene manner. The Third Plebeian, he who after listening to Brutus in scene two had agreed that Caesar was a tyrant and that 'We are blest that Rome is rid of him', is now crying out, 'Tear him, tear him!' The theatre audience of this performance are compelled, unless they shut their eyes and ears, to witness the consequences of Antony's rhetorical outburst: words kill. The impact of the juxtaposing of the action, and its subsequent consequences, is made all the more effective if, as I suspect Shakespeare hoped, many of the audience have allowed themselves to be moved by what Mark Antony said, or certainly by the *manner* in which he said it. Now, as a result, they not only have to witness the terrible subsequent events, but share in a collective sense of guilt and shame that comes from their knowledge that they have been susceptible to emotional manipulation. The immediate juxtaposing enables the audience to make the connection between the powerful but controlled rhetoric of scene two, and the terrible and uncontrolled violence it provokes in scene three.

Thus far in this chapter we have focused intensively on Shakespeare, but I want to take a further look at the importance in dramatic writing of juxtaposing by shifting that focus from the seventeenth to the twentieth century. The contemporary English dramatist, Edward Bond, wrote a now-famous play in the mid-nineteen-sixties called *Saved*. One scene in the play, in particular, caused much offence to those who saw it in performance, and even more to those who did not see it but heard about it from those who had. *Saved* is a play about the brutalization of the human spirit by an oppressive and institutionally violent society. The scene that caused such a furore (scene six) showed a group of young men murdering a baby in its pram. The scene is written in such a way as to emphasize the horrific detail of an act that happens because those involved cannot see the child they kill as anything other than an object – a thing, not a person. Although what is intended to be shown in the action is no worse than what is reported on a daily basis, and in graphic detail, in the popular press, the representation of the act of murdering a child on stage understandably upset a great many people. Of course, the experience of watching that simulated, but horrifyingly realistic, stoning of a small child is hard to bear in the theatre, or on the page. However, the text is controlled: it is designed and structured in such a way as not just to make an audience *share* a terrible experience – there is no point in simply doing that – but to make them *understand* it. Understanding comes, if it comes at all, from the juxtaposing of that event with what Bond chooses to present immediately after. Scene seven is set in a prison cell. In his printed foreword to the text, Bond stresses the need for the stage, throughout the action, to be 'as bare as possible – sometimes completely bare'. Not only does this put the focus on to the language of the actors but, as in Shakespeare, it allows the action to proceed uninterrupted by changes of scenery. It is vital that scene seven follows on immediately from six, just as it was that three should immediately be seen after two in *Julius Caesar*. In both plays, the action of the former scene is held up to the eyes and ears of the audience in order that they can make a comparison with the *reaction* of the latter. In *Saved*, scene seven, following the murder, one of those involved (it was a group act with no one individual solely responsible) enters. The stage directions state

A cell. Left centre a box to sit on. Otherwise, the stage is bare. A steel door bangs. FRED comes in from the left. He has a mac over his head. He sits on the case. After a slight pause he takes off the mac.

Silence. A steel door bangs. PAM comes in left.

The entry of Fred has been preceded by off-stage noises from an angry and violent crowd. Their cries mirror some of the tension and emotion in the theatre audience. The young man is seen to be covered in excreta; he has been kicked and spat upon by the crowd. There is the sound, repeated three times during the scene, of a heavy steel door slamming shut.

The juxtaposing of the two scenes shows a number of things. First, the audience were witnesses of the preceding scene, and therefore know how essentially futile and unrelated to reality is what happens as a result in the next. In scene seven, Fred, although he is far from being alone in his responsibility, offers a convenient way of discharging any sense of collective guilt by providing a subject to receive punishment. Second, the scene in prison presents yet another form of violence done to the person. The hatred directed towards Fred by the off-stage crowd (and by implication by the audience themselves), and their action in spitting at him and kicking him – their obvious desire to destroy him – parallels the action of the young men in scene six directing their hatred against a helpless victim. Both actions are equally pointless and savage. Lastly the sound of the door slamming shut is an aural metaphor for what has just occurred in the theatre to most of the audience, and what continually happens in 'real life'; anything that challenges our casual acceptance of the world as we want to believe it to be is, literally and metaphorically, shut out.

2 The Performer's Text

In the first part of this chapter, I want to concentrate on reading a text written by a dramatist as if engaged in directing it for the theatre. Our task is to manufacture a director's text. Before the actors, stage-management, designers, and technicians begin to formulate their texts, the director will already have taken decisions that will often radically affect both the development of those other texts during the forthcoming rehearsal process, and their eventual articulation before an audience. The modern theatre director is a figure who exercises very considerable power and influence over the theatrical product, greater in most cases than any other single individual, including the dramatist. Not everyone involved, including many actors and actresses, are happy with this situation; none the less, it persists. Historically of course, the director is a relative newcomer to theatre practice. Shakespeare's theatre had no one individual with sole responsibility for overseeing and controlling what an audience would eventually see in performance. The theatrical conditions of the day (absolutely minimal rehearsal time and a vast repertory of plays) did not permit the luxury of supporting someone who did not contribute to the work of the company either as a writer or, more usually, as an actor. In any case, direction in the sense of encouraging a particular *interpretation* of the dramatist's text, was considered neither practicable nor relevant. A leading player, such as Burbage, may have given minimal practical instruction to his fellow players in matters where it was required in order to prevent confusion on the playing-area. Among these would feature the timing of entrances and exits, the grouping of the actors at particular moments, and minor stage-business, but this is *staging* not directing. Not until the middle of the nineteenth century does any one individual begin to emerge as anything approaching the prototype of the modern director, and certainly the pre-eminence now enjoyed by many modern directors and the status their role carries with it is largely a phenomenon of the last twenty-five years. For better or for worse, our theatre practice is now director-dominated. It is in the director's mind that initial presentational strategies are charted.

The Director

From the moment directors decide or are appointed to direct plays, they do so in the light of particular circumstances that will inevitably limit their creative freedom of action. The amount of money available for the production is often the single most limiting factor. As readers in an ideal production situation (that is, an imaginary production) we are not hedged about by financial constraints, and cost need not concern us. What we should pay attention to are the less obvious, but no less significant constraints imposed by the availability to the director of individuals, notably of particular actors and actresses, and the playing space or theatre in which the eventual performance will be staged. Both these factors are known to the director before the rehearsals begin, and both will significantly modify his or her ideas on the presentation of the performance text. You, of course, have total freedom to stage your play in any environment you think appropriate and dramatically interesting, and also to choose to work with whomever you like on your imagined text-into-performance. But whatever you do, you cannot begin to realize fully your active reader's text unless you deliberately and consciously consider the environment in which that text is to be staged and how you are going to cast it.

Casting

Casting particular actors and actresses is a task that cannot be avoided in the theatre, and should not be avoided by the active reader of plays. It is a minefield through which to tread with extreme care, using intuition as well as reason for a guide. It is a process in which subjective judgements and prejudices are rife. Thinking for a moment about how we assess people when we meet them for the first time may help us to see more clearly some of the problems and challenges presented to a director when casting a play. When we meet strangers we try to 'read' them. They generate a whole series of visual and aural signs which we interpret and filter through our own particular set of prejudices. We observe their clothes and how they are worn, their hair, and general physical characteristics; are they fat, thin, tall and so on? We listen to their speech; to accent, to the tone and pitch of voice. From these, and many more impulses, we construct a highly personal but powerful first impression of what people are like. These impressions are, of course, coloured and formed by social attitudes and biases to which we are all prone. In other words, we use a kind of mental shorthand to sum up people. But the resulting stereotypes are not adequate when we meet, as directors, the characters on the printed page.

If a dramatist's text indicates clearly and unambiguously that a character possesses specific physical characteristics these must be respected. For example, in Shakespeare's *A Midsummer Night's Dream*, the actress chosen to play Helena should be taller than the one to play Hermia: the former is referred to as a 'painted maypole' (Act III, Scene ii, line 296) and the latter as 'low' and 'little' (Act III, Scene ii, line 326). In such a case the task of casting the roles has partially been done. Rarely is a dramatist's text so helpful and explicit. As soon as highly subjective terms such as 'beautiful' or 'ugly' or 'plain' are applied to characters in a play, either by the dramatist or by one of the dramatist's characters, then the real issues and problems of casting begin.

When casting a play in the imagination, care must be taken to examine the appropriateness of the immediate images of individual characters which spring to mind. We have to slow things down to explore what is almost certainly a crude stereotype. We create these images in our mind's eye whatever we do; the point is consciously and carefully to consider what the imagination offers up as an immediate response to the signals emitted from a dramatist's text. What does and, in the context of the play as a whole, should signify 'beauty'? How old is 'old'? We must be prepared to challenge our own preconceptions as we read, and in particular to be sure to ask how, in the practice of casting, we are applying these terms, and to what extent our evidence for their use is reliable and appropriate. To choose a real or an imagined actor or actress for a particular role is to make a statement. It not only indicates confidence in him or her to perform in a particular way, but also your commitment to an idea of how you see the character to be portrayed. Casting decisions can affect significantly the overall interpretation of the performance text that will be available to an audience.

In his production of Shakespeare's *The Tempest* for the National Theatre, the director, Peter Hall, cast the actor Michael Feast as Ariel. The director's text that Hall was in the business of making seemed to him to require an Ariel who was 'sexless'; therefore Michael Feast was chosen because of what Peter Hall perceived as his androgynous quality. In the same play, he made a similar (critical) decision regarding the casting of Ferdinand and Miranda: that they 'should of course be very young'.[3] But there is no 'of course'! Hall's decision as to how to cast all three roles is both legitimate and necessary, but it is a subjective, evaluative statement about *his* text at a particular but crucial moment in its genesis.

Terry Hands, the co-director of the Royal Shakespeare Company, considers casting a play one of the most difficult and important tasks that falls to a modern director. He provided a good example of effective casting in his 1980 production for the RSC of Shakespeare's *Richard II*. His choice of Alan Howard as Richard, and David Suchet as Bolingbroke/Henry IV, made possible and credible a director's text which articulated in performance two very different and conflicting statements about kinship and the exercise of political power which are both present in the dramatist's text. Often it is necessary to treat these opposed elements of the play as mutually exclusive, so Hand's inspired casting provided an extremely subtle and effective aspect to his director's text. Alan Howard is a tall, physically lithe and elegant actor, with blond hair, blue eyes, and a fine ringing voice: an actor very capable of projecting the image of a heroic stereotype. His Richard was a kind of medieval icon, of whom it was easy for the audience to believe he was 'not born to sue, but to command' (Act I, Scene i, line 196). Alan Howard's actor's text showed a king in love with his own public image; an image built upon complete familiarity and ease with the exploitation of public ceremony and ritual. Watching Richard in the play's early ceremonial scenes, the audience in the theatre had no difficulty in understanding the latter remark of York, on the occasion of Richard's return from Ireland and subsequent confrontation with the revolt led by Bolingbroke:

Yet looks he like a king. Behold, his eye,
As bright as is the eagle's, lightens forth
Controlling majesty. Alack, alack for woe
That any harm should stain so fair a show!
(III, iii, lines 68–71)

The traumatic events of Richard's eventual deposition were felt by the audience through their own loss of the thrill and excitement they had experienced from watching a spectacle tremendously and *fittingly* well done.

David Suchet's Bolingbroke, on the other hand, was presented both through appearance and interpretation, as a very different character. Suchet is short, dark and stockily built. He lacks the flamboyance of Alan Howard, and is less immediately physically impressive. In his actor's text, the role of Henry IV showed a man who ruled through a grasp of the political rather than the ceremonial world. David Suchet's Henry, unlike Howard's Richard, was a man more at home behind a desk than on a throne. Indeed, in Terry Hand's production, the new Henry IV was so unsure of how to wear the crown that he chose to keep it on a desk in front of him rather than on his head.

In the 1950s, Laurence Olivier made a film version of his highly acclaimed Old Vic staging of Shakespeare's *Richard III*. It is a film that has subsequently become justifiably famous and has served as an introduction to Shakespeare in performance for many schoolchildren. Olivier cast himself as Richard, Duke of Gloucester, and in the minor but significant role of Lady Anne, he made a change from the casting of the staged version of the play to include a new actress in the role: the young and very beautiful Claire Bloom. One of the most famous scenes in the play, and one of the most memorable in the film, is the so-called 'wooing scene' (Act I, Scene ii). In Shakespeare's text, Richard confronts Lady Anne over the dead body of her father-in-law Henry VI, whom he has killed, and whom she is escorting to his burial. Richard has also been responsible for the death of her husband. Anne is fully aware of what Richard has done, but despite these apparently insurmountable odds, by the end of the scene (less than ten minutes' playing time), Richard seems to have succeeded in winning a promise from her, not only of forgiveness, but also of future love. Do read the scene before you go on.

> *Enter the corse of Henry the Sixth, with halberds to guard it; Lady Anne being the mourner, attended by Tressel and Berkeley*

ANNE:
    Set down, set down your honourable load –
    If honour may be shrouded in a hearse –
    Whilst I awhile obsequiously lament
    Th'untimely fall of virtuous Lancaster.
        The bearers set down the hearse
    Poor key-cold figure of a holy king,
    Pale ashes of the house of Lancaster,
    Thou bloodless remnant of that royal blood,
    Be it lawful that I invocate thy ghost
    To hear the lamentations of poor Anne,
    Wife to thy Edward, to thy slaughtered son   10
    Stabbed by the selfsame hand that made these wounds!
    Lo, in these windows that let forth thy life
    I pour the helpless balm of my poor eyes.
    O, cursèd be the hand that made these holes!
    Cursèd the heart that had the heart to do it!
    Cursèd the blood that let this blood from hence!
    More direful hap betide that hated wretch
    That makes us wretched by the death of thee
    Than I can wish to wolves – to spiders, toads,
    Or any creeping venomed thing that lives!   20
    If ever he have child, abortive be it,
    Prodigious, and untimely brought to light,
    Whose ugly and unnatural aspect
    May fright the hopeful mother at the view,
    And that be heir to his unhappiness!
    If ever he have wife, let her be made
    More miserable by the life of him

Than I am made by my young lord and thee!
Come now, towards Chertsey with your holy load,
Taken from Paul's to be interrèd there.   30

    The bearers take up the hearse

And still, as you are weary of this weight,
Rest you, whiles I lament King Henry's corse.

    Enter Richard, Duke of Gloucester

RICHARD:

Stay, you that bear the corse, and set it down.

ANNE:

What black magician conjures up this fiend
To stop devoted charitable deeds?

RICHARD:

Villains, set down the corse, or, by Saint Paul,
I'll make a corse of him that disobeys!

GENTLEMAN:

My lord, stand back, and let the coffin pass.

RICHARD:

Unmannered dog! Stand thou, when I command!
Advance thy halberd higher than my breast,   40
Or, by Saint Paul, I'll strike thee to my foot
And spurn upon thee, beggar, for thy boldness.

    The bearers set down the hearse

ANNE:

What, do you tremble? Are you all afraid?
Alas, I blame you not, for you are mortal,
And mortal eyes cannot endure the devil.
Avaunt, thou dreadful minister of hell!
Thou hadst but power over his mortal body;
His soul thou canst not have. Therefore, be gone.

RICHARD:

Sweet saint, for charity, be not so curst.

ANNE:

Foul devil, for God's sake hence, and trouble us not,   50
For thou hast made the happy earth thy hell,
Filled it with cursing cries and deep exclaims.
If thou delight to view thy heinous deeds,
Behold this pattern of thy butcheries.
O gentlemen, see, see! Dead Henry's wounds
Open their congealed mouths and bleed afresh!
Blush, blush, thou lump of foul deformity;
For 'tis thy presence that exhales this blood
From cold and empty veins where no blood dwells.
Thy deed inhuman and unnatural   60
Provokes this deluge most unnatural.

O God, which this blood mad'st, revenge his death!
O earth, which this blood drink'st, revenge his death!
Either heaven with lightning strike the murderer dead;
Or earth gape open wide and eat him quick,
As thou dost swallow up this good King's blood
Which his hell-governed arm hath butcherèd!

RICHARD:
Lady, you know no rules of charity,
Which renders good for bad, blessings for curses.

ANNE:
Villain, thou know'st nor law of God nor man: 70
No beast so fierce but knows some touch of pity.

RICHARD:
But I know none, and therefore am no beast.

ANNE:
O wonderful, when devils tell the truth!

RICHARD:
More wonderful, when angels are so angry.
Vouchsafe, divine perfection of a woman,
Of these supposèd crimes to give me leave
By circumstance but to acquit myself.

ANNE:
Vouchsafe, diffused infection of a man,
Of these known evils, but to give me leave
By circumstance to accuse thy cursèd self.   80

RICHARD:
Fairer than tongue can name thee, let me have
Some patient leisure to excuse myself.

ANNE:
Fouler than heart can think thee, thou canst make
No excuse current but to hang thyself.

RICHARD:
By such despair I should accuse myself.

ANNE:
And by despairing shalt thou stand excused
For doing worthy vengeance on thyself
That didst unworthy slaughter upon others.

RICHARD:
Say that I slew them not.

ANNE: Then say they were not slain.
But dead they are, and, devilish slave, by thee.   90

RICHARD:
I did not kill your husband.

ANNE: Why, then he is alive.

45

RICHARD:

Nay, he is dead, and slain by Edward's hands.

ANNE:

In thy foul throat thou li'st! Queen Margaret saw
Thy murderous falchion smoking in his blood;
The which thou once didst bend against her breast,
But that thy brothers beat aside the point.

RICHARD:

I was provokèd by her slanderous tongue
That laid their guilt upon my guiltless shoulders.

ANNE:

Thou wast provokèd by thy bloody mind
That never dream'st on aught but butcheries.   100
Didst thou not kill this King?

RICHARD: I grant ye – yea.

ANNE:

Dost grant me, hedgehog? Then God grant me too
Thou mayst be damnèd for that wicked deed!
O, he was gentle, mild, and virtuous!

RICHARD:

The better for the King of Heaven that hath him.

ANNE:

He is in heaven, where thou shalt never come.

RICHARD:

Let him thank me that holp to send him thither;
For he was fitter for that place than earth.

ANNE:

And thou unfit for any place, but hell.

RICHARD:

Yes, one place else, if you will hear me name it.   110

ANNE:

Some dungeon.

RICHARD: Your bedchamber.

ANNE:

Ill rest betide the chamber where thou liest!

RICHARD:

So will it, madam, till I lie with you.

ANNE:

I hope so.

RICHARD: I know so. But, gentle Lady Anne,
To leave this keen encounter of our wits
And fall something into a slower method,
Is not the causer of the timeless deaths
Of these Plantagenets, Henry and Edward,
As blameful as the executioner?

ANNE:

Thou wast the cause and most accursed effect. 120

RICHARD:

Your beauty was the cause of that effect –
Your beauty, that did haunt me in my sleep
To undertake the death of all the world,
So I might live one hour in your sweet bosom.

ANNE:

If I thought that, I tell thee, homicide,
These nails should rent that beauty from my cheeks.

RICHARD:

These eyes could not endure that beauty's wrack;
You should not blemish it, if I stood by.
As all the world is cheerèd by the sun,
So I by that. It is my day, my life. 130

ANNE:

Black night o'ershade thy day, and death thy life!

RICHARD:

Curse not thyself, fair creature – thou art both.

ANNE:

I would I were, to be revenged on thee.

RICHARD:

It is a quarrel most unnatural
To be revenged on him that loveth thee.

ANNE:

It is a quarrel just and reasonable
To be revenged on him that killed my husband.

RICHARD:

He that bereft thee, lady, of thy husband
Did it to help thee to a better husband.

ANNE:

His better doth not breathe upon the earth. 140

RICHARD:

He lives, that loves thee better than he could.

ANNE:

Name him.

RICHARD: Plantagenet.

ANNE:

                    Why that was he.

RICHARD:

The selfsame name, but one of better nature.

ANNE:

Where is he?

RICHARD: Here.

        She spits at him

Why dost thou spit at me?

ANNE:

Would it were mortal poison for thy sake!

RICHARD:

Never came poison from so sweet a place.

ANNE:

Never hung poison on a fouler toad.

Out of my sight! Thou dost infect mine eyes.

RICHARD:

Thine eyes, sweet lady, have infected mine.

ANNE:

Would they were basilisks to strike thee dead!   150

RICHARD:

I would they were, that I might die at once,
For now they kill me with a living death.
Those eyes of thine from mine have drawn salt tears,
Shamed their aspects with store of childish drops.
These eyes, which never shed remorseful tear –
No, when my father York and Edward wept
To hear the piteous moan that Rutland made
When black-faced Clifford shook his sword at him;
Nor when thy warlike father, like a child,
Told the sad story of my father's death   160
And twenty times made pause to sob and weep,
That all the standers-by had wet their cheeks
Like trees bedashed with rain – in that sad time
My manly eyes did scorn an humble tear;
And what these sorrows could not thence exhale,
Thy beauty hath, and made them blind with weeping.
I never sued to friend nor enemy;
My tongue could never learn sweet smoothing word;
But, now thy beauty is proposed my fee,
My proud heart sues, and prompts my tongue to speak.   170
    She looks scornfully at him
Teach not thy lip such scorn; for it was made
For kissing, lady, not for such contempt.
If thy revengeful heart cannot forgive,
Lo, here I lend thee this sharp-pointed sword,
Which if thou please to hide in this true breast
And let the soul forth that adoreth thee,
I lay it naked to the deadly stroke
And humbly beg the death upon my knee.
    He lays his breast open. She offers at it with his sword
Nay, do not pause; for I did kill King Henry –
But 'twas thy beauty that provokèd me.   180

Nay now, dispatch; 'twas I that stabbed young Edward –
But 'twas thy heavenly face that set me on.
> *She falls the sword*
Take up the sword again, or take up me.

ANNE:
Arise, dissembler; though I wish thy death
I will not be thy executioner.

RICHARD:
Then bid me kill myself, and I will do it.

ANNE:
I have already.

RICHARD: That was in thy rage.
Speak it again, and even with the word
This hand, which for thy love did kill thy love,
Shall for thy love kill a far truer love;   190
To both their deaths shalt thou be accessory.

ANNE:
I would I knew thy heart.

RICHARD:
'Tis figured in my tongue.

ANNE:
I fear me both are false.

RICHARD:
Then never was man true.

ANNE:
Well, well, put up your sword.

RICHARD:
Say then my peace is made.

ANNE:
That shalt thou know hereafter.

RICHARD:
But shall I live in hope?

ANNE:
All men, I hope, live so.   200

RICHARD:
Vouchsafe to wear this ring.

ANNE:
To take is not to give.
> *She puts on the ring*

RICHARD:
Look how my ring encompasseth thy finger,
Even so thy breast encloseth my poor heart.
Wear both of them, for both of them are thine;
And if thy poor devoted servant may
But beg one favour at thy gracious hand,

Thou dost confirm his happiness for ever.

ANNE:

What is it?

RICHARD:

That it may please you leave these sad designs   210
To him that hath more cause to be a mourner,
And presently repair to Crosby House;
Where, after I have solemnly interred
At Chertsey monastery this noble king
And wet his grave with my repentant tears,
I will with all expedient duty see you.
For divers unknown reasons, I beseech you,
Grant me this boon.

ANNE:

With all my heart; and much it joys me too.
To see you are become so penitent.   220
Tressel and Berkeley, go along with me.

RICHARD:

Bid me farewell.

ANNE: 'Tis more than you deserve;
But since you teach me how to flatter you,
Imagine I have said farewell already.

Exeunt Tressel and Berkeley, with Anne

RICHARD:

Sirs, take up the corse.

GENTLEMAN: Towards Chertsey, noble lord?

RICHARD:

No, to Whitefriars – there attend my coming.

Exeunt bearers and guard with corse

The scene as Shakespeare wrote it must have appeared to Olivier to be asking far too much of a cinema audience by expecting them to believe in the credibility of the action it relates. In fact, Olivier exacerbated the potential problem of belief in Richard's actions by changing the dramatist's text to make the corpse not that of Anne's father-in-law but that of her husband! What Olivier obviously wanted to emphasize in *his* text of director *and* actor was Richard's ability as a lover: the prize was great, and the barriers to its possession enormous. To give this scenario a chance of appearing convincing, he had to further change Shakespeare's text. He split the wooing scene into two distinct halves by inserting an earlier episode, in which Clarence is led off to the Tower, at the point where Anne exhibited the first signs of a change in her attitude to Richard. The break in the scene was obviously intended to give psychological credibility to Richard and Anne's extraordinary actions. But are these actions really so difficult to accept in performance? Given Shakespeare's text, and not Olivier's, there is, I think, no problem if Lady Anne is properly cast.

Claire Bloom was not only beautiful, she also displayed a strong aura of self-confidence and maturity. But the more impressive the physical presence of the actress playing Anne, the greater will be the audience's difficulty in accepting her seduction as believable and consistent with her character. If you think for a moment that this scene shows events at a funeral, you might recall that on such occasions, those most nearly involved with the dead person are extremely vulnerable. They may need, and they may seek, consolation where they can find it, for it is an occasion characterized by emotional turmoil and confusion. If, in the role of Anne, an actress is cast who looks young – perhaps very young, say fifteen or sixteen – and who is also physically slight and not especially beautiful (we have only Richard's evidence to indicate her physical qualities, and he is hardly the most reliable source), then immediately the scope for a display by Anne of her real vulnerability will have been greatly enhanced.

When you come to cast this role, you should extend your imaginative casting of this scene to include all the other characters in it. When this is done, an interpretation emphasizing Anne's vulnerability is strengthened. The corpse is borne by pall-bearers and guarded. There are also two silent, but named characters: Tressel and Berkeley. If all these men are played by tall and powerfully built actors, then what the audience sees is a spectacle in which a very young woman is isolated and vulnerable. She is the only woman, and she has no allies. Yet this, the least physically impressive person on stage, has the most difficult task to enact. It is *her* difficulty that this casting emphasizes; not Richard's difficulty in wooing her. Lady Anne must both bury a King, and publicly 'obsequiously lament[ing] Th'untimely fall of virtuous Lancaster'. For Laurence Olivier's Richard successfully to seduce Claire Bloom's Lady Anne in the time given by Shakespeare in his text, might well have failed to convince an audience. But, had Olivier's Richard been seen to seduce a near-child at a funeral, his soliloquy at the end of the scene, 'Was ever woman in this humour wooed?/Was ever woman in this humour won?' would have had a hollow rather than a victorious ring to it. For what the audience could see in this scene, and can see only if it is appropriately cast, is a conflict in which the eventual 'victory' is negligible because the battle was between vastly unequal forces. This interpretation can be reinforced by careful choice of properties, and by using the large number of silent characters indicated in the printed text. We will return to this scene again later in the book.

Deliberately and consciously casting a play as you read it is almost always a profitable exercise. Although it can be a difficult task, the problems faced are nothing when compared to those you will encounter if, in your director's text, you find it necessary, as Olivier did, to cut or adapt a dramatist's text. It is common practice in the professional theatre, particularly in the production of classic plays, for a director to change what a dramatist has written, or at least to change what has been printed or what a dramatist is *thought* to have written, by the omission of some part of it, or even by the addition of new material. John Barton, in his work as a director for the RSC, has sometimes aroused the wrath and indignation of a section of critical opinion by his habit of adding to Shakespeare's text portions written by himself, and by taking selected extracts from other Shakespeare plays and incorporating them into different productions. Of course if you, as a student of dramatic literature, suddenly begin to re-write Shakespeare, you may be in trouble. There is, however, an equal danger in an over-reverential attitude to Shakespeare's plays which can inhibit the necessary creative thinking required to move from printed text into performance text.

Theatrical Fidelity

The competing claims for the authority of different texts (for example of directors, dramatists, actors and designers) raises the issue of theatrical fidelity: what should constitute a legitimate interpretation of a printed text by an active reader of plays? How much freedom should students of dramatic literature allow themselves in making an imaginary performance text? It is impossible to give a definitive answer. Many of those who interpret plays in the theatre argue for absolute freedom to use a dramatist's text in any way they see fit. They argue that the criteria for judging the legitimacy of the exercise should be theatrical, not literary. In other words, if an idea is thought to work in performance, it is legitimate. For the active reader, the argument essentially concerns the extent of authority given the dramatist, as there is no audience, other than himself or herself to applaud or dispute an imaginary production. The line should be drawn, I think, at re-writing parts of a play, despite the fact that there is good evidence that this was common practice in the Elizabethan and Jacobean theatre. If, for example, in your interpretation of *King Lear* you decide to cast the King with an actor in his forties because you want to stress that his abdication is not the action of a semi-senile old man but of one freely opting for the pleasures of early retirement, eventually you will come up against a line in the printed text that states Lear's age:

KING LEAR: I am a very foolish fond old man,
    Fourscore and upward.
            (IV,vii, lines 60–61)

How old is old is here answered clearly: over eighty. The only way around this fact is to omit the line or re-write it. Even if we stop short at rewriting a dramatist's text, there remains open an enormous range of creative interpretations, some of which may arouse the anguished cries of those who seek to defend the dramatist's right to self-expression.

One of the most common forms of textual adaption by a director is to make a change in the historical period in which a play has been located by its author. For example, Jonathan Miller set a production of Shakespeare's *The Merchant of Venice* in the late nineteenth century. Presumably he chose to do this because he felt that by setting the action in an era historically associated in the public imagination with a devotion to highly competitive business and commerce, he was showing a *greater* fidelity to Shakespeare's text than leaving the action in a rather vague Elizabethan 'Venetian' location, thought of as picturesque. Another interpretative idea by this same director aroused an interesting argument recorded in the published diaries of Sir Peter Hall. Hall, Miller and the playwright Harold Pinter were discussing Miller's proposal to stage Oscar Wilde's *The Importance of Being Earnest* with an all-male cast.

There was a sharp division between Jonathan and Harold Pinter. Pinter's position is clear: an author has certain clear intentions, and Wilde's intentions were not that women should be played by men. Jonathan asserted repeatedly that it was a director's right to re-interpret a play in any way that seemed significant to him, once the play was no longer new. He was making a fool of nobody but himself, and the play was still there at the end of the day. Harold feels one has a greater responsibility to a dead dramatist than to a living one.[4]

It is really a matter of balance and degree. If writers want total control over what they produce, then they should write novels or make films, not write plays. In any case what is performed in the theatre is, by contrast to what has been written and set down, ephemeral. Even so, directors can make fools of far more people than themselves, beginning with their actors. There is undeniably a continuing tension between contemporary directors and dramatists. Some, like Edward Bond, have to some extent controlled the staging of their work by directing it themselves. Others, Harold Pinter for example, have established an understanding with a particular director (Peter Hall) as to the extent and nature of their creative collaboration.

The tension is not a recent phenomenon, only the form in which it manifests itself is new. In the nineteenth century, the argument was between the rights of the dramatist and those of the actor, and the actor-manager in particular. Shakespeare was subject to extensive cutting. The great Sir Henry Irving cut *The Merchant of Venice* following Shylock's final departure in the trial scene (he was playing Shylock), thus omitting the whole of the fifth act. George Bernard Shaw, in his role as critic, tried to defend his fellow writers against the practices of actor-managers like Beerbohm-Tree, who, Shaw claimed, far from being content with cutting plays, disembowelled them. But the practice persisted, aided and abetted by the demands of designers who created enormous and spectacularly realistic settings which took a great deal of time to change, and were therefore *only* changed when it became absolutely unavoidable.

Norman Marshall in *The Producer and the Play* gives a wonderful example of just what could be done to a dramatist's text by a determined assault on it through the demands of nineteenth-century spectacular staging:

He [Augustin Daly, manager of Her Majesty's Theatre] began with the first scene of the second act [of Shakespeare's *Twelfth Night*] – the landing of Antonio and Sebastian. 'This rearrangement,' explained one of the critics, 'although it destroys all dramatic suspense as to the fate of Viola's brother, has the advantage of allowing the star (Miss Rehan) to enter after the audience is seated.' To make things easier for the scene-shifters, the second scene of the first act was played next. Then the sea-coast scene was got out of the way and the Duke's palace was revealed, a fine, elaborate set – so elaborate that there it had to stay for the rest of the act. Daly got out of this difficulty by what one critic described as 'a bold rearrangement of the text'. The first and fourth scenes of Act I were played consecutively as a single scene; then, after the curtain had been lowered for a moment to denote a passage of time, scenes three and five of Act I were joined together with the second scene of Act II, all run together without a break.[5]

In the nineteenth century, therefore, in Britain, the dramatist's text was generally subservient to the demands of those of actor and designer, and it certainly carried less status in performance. In Britain at any rate, this was the age of the novel as far as most creative writers were concerned.

Ultimately you, as an active reader, have to decide for yourself what will constitute your imagined performance-text, and how you will organize and balance the textual statements coming from all the various textual perspectives involved in making a performance. Remember no master-text exists for a performance (nor indeed is there really any master-study that can show you the way to manufacture it). All you can do is to make your own decisions in the light of your knowledge and of the fact that there are no right answers, only good arguments. These arguments, and the necessary risk-taking they involve, must be expressed in theatrical, and not exclusively literary, critical terms.

The Actor

As we have seen, the dramatist makes a blueprint for further action, and the director goes to work using it as a basis for a presentational strategy which will be tried and tested in the rehearsal room, and ultimately in performance. But almost the last people to become involved in the process of making text-into-performance are the actors, without whose skills and insight the ideas of the playwright will remain on the page or in the imagination. For better or for worse, the theatre in Great Britain in the 1980s is not primarily an actor's theatre. As a group involved in the production process they exercise relatively little power and control over either the choice of material, or the eventual outcome of their collective labours in the shape of a performance. We produce, as a nation, many very successful actors and actresses whose work is admired throughout much of the world, but their status in the production collective is low. The actual process of rehearsal, the time in which ideas are shaped, taken up and discarded, is in the control of the director, and the performance text itself is very often circumscribed by decisions taken by directors (and designers) long before the first actor gets hold of the printed text from which his or her work is to begin. His or her perception of that text is, to some extent, mediated by the actions and reactions of the director. I think it is true to say that the product of much of the so-called legitimate theatre (and by that I mean large, state-subsidized companies) is designed to be appreciated by its audience intellectually and cerebrally, rather than sensuously or experientially. Of course that is not to say that contemporary theatrical experience is devoid of emotion and sensuality. Indeed, as we have seen, atmosphere and mood – the two things that generate the tension between observer and observed in a performance-text – are perceived and appreciated through the emotions and the senses, and not only through the intellect. But the full power latent in the actor's relationship to an audience, the power that is capable of creating an intense emotional experience, is not encountered on our stage as frequently as is the entertaining and cleverly animated lecture. Our theatre is, I think, primarily accorded merit and status in proportion to the extent to which it is a theatre of ideas.

The status accorded to the presentation of complex ideas which require sophisticated analytical skills on the part of the audience, affects dramatists and directors. It particularly increases the power of the director (who is today almost certainly a university graduate) over the actor (who is most often trained at drama school). At a university, as opposed to a drama school, *words* are the bricks that build an intellectual training. The ability to use words, to analyse and discuss ideas in spoken and written language, is *the* primary skill that most directors bring with them to their work. In all probability it is the skill that you too, as an active reader of plays, will bring to yours. It is not that the skill is inappropriate or unnecessary, far from it, but we need simply to state that the actor's path towards the creation of his or her text is not necessarily the same as that of the director. As Janet Suzman remarked:

... *talking about acting* is a contradiction in terms. Gesture, tones of voice, expressions in the eye, movements of the body, all these are quite beyond me to describe in words.[6]

And Cicely Berry, voice coach to the Royal Shakespeare Company, remarked very recently concerning her work with actors:

What interests me is the actual, *physical* nature of the text. When we talk, we rather think of it as being mainly to do with our heads. But language evolved from sounds we made to communicate our needs, and that's a very physical thing. We can still be upset by words, they can still have a physical effect on us which goes beyond simply how we're thinking.[7]

I am not trying to imply that one group is better equipped to make performances than the other. But the director's intellectual training has, presumably, given him or her skills of analysis and criticism considered inappropriate and sometimes irrelevant in the training of an actor. The current dominance of the director-as-intellectual is caught in a comment made by the critic and editor Stanley Wells of John Barton's production of Shakespeare's *Richard II* for the RSC. Wells speaks of Barton's

... dramatic method [which] throws an emphasis on ideas and their poetical expression rather than on credibility of action and psychologically plausible portrayal of individual personalities.[8]

It is not simply in the presentation of the classics that the intellectual approach flourishes. Theatre critics, who bear an enormous responsibility for what is actually shown on our stage both in terms of their response to new material and to the way in which they can make or break all but the strongest of theatrical reputations, appear biased towards a product the contents of which require evaluative skills of a kind they recognize as legitimate. I raise this issue because when you begin to consider the actor's text you must recognize that acting is not, primarily, an intellectual, or even a particularly self-analytical activity. Most actors will tell you that too much conscious thought about a character, too much 'intellectualizing', can actually become a barrier between the actor's own personality and that of the character he or she is seeking to become. I am aware, having used the word 'become' in that context, that there are other ways of approaching a role which are more concerned with 'showing' than with 'becoming' a character. But they are outside the mainstream tradition of acting in this country, where intuition and the surrender of self to character is more valued than is a self-conscious awareness of the mechanics of the process the actor is engaged in manufacturing.

It is interesting, I think, that the latter approach is defended (in a recently published book on acting) by a director, and the former by an actor. William Gaskill is the advocate of an *analytical*, Brechtian, approach to the enactment of a role, while the actor Simon Callow defends the legitimacy of an *emotional* identification of the actor and his character:

We argued especially about character. It was my deep conviction that all acting is rooted in character. It was a semi-Stanislavskian point of view, but mainly derived from the misery that I experienced as an actor until I had a firm grip on who I was in the play. Bill Gaskill counters by saying that character was a bourgeois concept based on identification. He said that for him who a character was was of no interest, only what he did. These discussions drove me back to the Messingkauf Dialogues of Brecht, which I now understand for the first time. If a play, says Brecht, is a report on an event, the audience only needs to know as much about the characters of the play as makes the event clear. I could see the force of that; but I knew in my heart exactly what kind of performances I liked to see.[9]

What contribution then, can the reader-as-actor make to the debate of text-into-performance which must, of course, be conducted as an analytical exercise? You must, I think, recognize and accept that the actor's part in the rehearsal debate may not necessarily be expressed in intellectual or critical terms, indeed may not be expressed orally at all. An actor makes meaning and articulates feelings through the whole body: through gestures, the voice, and an intuitive sense of what happens to *feel* right or true. The text being articulated owes as much to intuition as it does to intellect.[10] It is difficult for us as readers to emulate the actors' approach to their text, (we *have* to use words to express our ideas about the text) but we can and should none the less acknowledge that an actor's view of a character, and the questions that need to be asked, are often very different from those that tend to preoccupy a director.

Some actors will attempt to research a character by approaching it, as it were, from the inside out. They adopt the methods of a psychological detective, attempting to get inside the head of the character and look out at the world through his or her eyes. Other actors may seek to discover their roles from the outside in. They chose to adopt a particular physical characteristic (for example, Sir Laurence Olivier's now-legendary performance of Othello grew out of the actor's initial concern with the voice and movements of a Negro). The point is that actors are not like scholars. If you want to play Hamlet, it is not a prerequisite at audition to have read all, or most, of the recently published material about the play, or even to have read any. But it is a requirement to discover (and this is what you as reader *can* do) how the other characters think and feel about him, and, of course, how he thinks and feels about himself.

Janet Suzman, talking about playing Hedda Gabler in Ibsen's play of that name, serves as an interesting corrective to the reader who becomes too preoccupied with attempting to create an objective and critical overview of the whole of the events portrayed in the action of the text. A director must evolve a super-text, but the actor's concern is only with his or her character:

... to act a character is to be entirely partisan about that character. You must defend that character to the death. You must love her as you love yourself. You must, if necessary, loathe her as you loathe yourself.[11]

To make such an absolute identification is beyond most of us, but we can and should note once again that what preoccupies an actor and what preoccupies a director, are not the same. For instance, we can learn something from the questions Miss Suzman thought it appropriate to ask about Hedda; questions we would do well to ask of many characters, both male and female, and to recognize as significant starting points in building an actor's text:

What demon winds blew her about? What did she get hurt by? What defensive about? What did she love? What bored her? What excited her? When did she lie? When tell the truth? What made her laugh? What cry?[12]

In building up such a picture of a role, you as a reader-thinking-as-an actor, must take care to draw a distinction between what *you* know, given your overview of what the dramatist has written, and what your particular character or characters *can* know given their limited knowledge of the total events of a whole play. For example, when Hamlet goes off on his enforced journey to England, he is physically absent from the stage for almost an hour of playing time. It is therefore important to remember that if you are thinking as if you were the actor playing Hamlet, that you must exclude from your thoughts material that takes place during his absence that Hamlet cannot be aware of, and subsequently does not learn.

Silent Characters

When we are thinking about actors and about acting the text, let us remember as a first principle that any actor on-stage being observed by an audience is acting irrespective of whether or not he or she happens to be speaking. The significance of this simple fact (that acting is more than talking) is sometimes forgotten when reading a dramatist's text. Indeed, whenever we are studying the manufacture of text-into-performance it is necessary to remember that the dramatic significance of a character cannot automatically be measured by the number of words he or she is given to speak. The active reader must try to recall and visualize the totality of the enactment of a role in performance.

To do this, the reader starts by acknowledging the importance for actors of being able to listen to other actors speaking. The enactment of listening in a performance text can be of equal importance as an expressive act as talking. When we read what the dramatist's text gives character A to say, we cannot understand fully the meaning of what is said solely by analysis, however thorough, of the spoken text. We must look to see to whom A's text is addressed. Now B (the addressee) generates a text through his or her response to what he or she hears. That reaction, generated through body-language or gestural action, may well influence what A says, and the manner in which it is said. Although A is speaking the dramatist's text that you can *read*, B is just as significantly articulating a response that you need to *see* in your mind's eye if you are to understand the complete exchange. Indeed, as far as the audience are concerned, neither of the two actors is speaking *the* text, because that is what the audience themselves are making by observing the activity of the actors and making significance out of it.

You can, of course, further extend this process of making a performance text. Suppose the discussion of A and B is overheard by a third actor. The role of this figure may not be clear (you may indeed have missed his entrance in the list of characters indicated on the printed page), but if he is present on-stage, you cannot ignore him, for he too is contributing to the totality of the textual statement of a performance text. You must *decide* if C is visible to the audience, if he is seen by A and B, or by one or neither of them. Can C overhear what is being said by A, and is A's text modified as a result? How does C react to what he observes; does his reaction further condition the text of the audience, and if so, in what way? These, and other factors of so-called silent characters (B and C), should serve to make us aware that what is said in performance and what is meant, do not always correspond. The reader who accepts dialogue at face value, or reads only with knowledge of the conventions of non-dramatic literature, can all too easily miss many instances of which this is true. When reading a play, the focus of attention is almost inevitably on the words being spoken by what seem to be the principal characters in the drama, but as we have already seen, you cannot necessarily judge the dramatic significance of an actor's role by what is printed in the dramatist's text for him or her to say. Further exploration of the role of actors in a performance text who appear to have very little to say (and in some cases nothing at all) demonstrates the fruitfulness of considering the function of silent characters.

If we go back to the wooing scene in *Richard III*, we will find a good example of the potential power of silent characters to articulate a text, and of the need for the reader to take positive decisions to facilitate an imaginary enactment of that text. This scene is a classic case of action that cannot begin to be fully comprehended by the reader unless that reader is prepared to activate his or her imagination and take up the creative challenge offered to it.

In the Penguin edition of *Richard III* appears the following directions:

Enter the corse of Henry the Sixth, with halberds to guard it; Lady Anne being the mourner.

Now the corpse of the dead king (played presumably by an actor and not by a dummy) cannot walk on to the stage, and it will therefore need to be carried by at least six actors. The directions specify that the corpse is guarded; it therefore seems reasonable to suppose that those who carry the body of the dead king are in no position to guard it, and that we therefore require another group of actors to enact the guard. You must decide how many guards guard the funeral procession of a dead king. Shakespeare himself may have been thinking of the historical evidence contained in Edward Hall's *The Union of the Noble and Illustre Famelies of Lancastre and York*, published in 1548. In this history the funeral of Henry VI is described as a poor affair.

without Priest or Clarke, Torche or Taper,
syngyn or saiyng ...

Given this, and the relatively small numbers of actors employed by an Elizabethan company, plus the fact that Lady Anne is the only person of rank and status in society to be present, let us suppose that there are six halberds to guard the corpse (not many when you think of state funerals). Although the opening directions don't refer to them, two characters are mentioned by name in the subsequent spoken text: Tressel and Berkeley.

These two gentlemen enter with the funeral procession, making a cast of at least sixteen actors on-stage at the beginning of the scene: six pall-bearers, six halberds guarding the corpse, Lady Anne, Tressel and Berkeley, and the corpse of Henry VI. When the actor playing Richard enters the scene, you have a stage crowded with seventeen actors, and a printed text that is apparently only concerned with two.

Having noted the number of actors required for this scene, you now have to consider their significance. How do they enter the playing-area, and what impression are you seeking to communicate to an audience by your handling of that entry? At this point all *I* can do is what I hope *you* will also do – but for yourself, in your own terms that is, begin to animate the text.

Let us say that the procession is formal and solemn. There is no music to accompany the entrance, and the very silence creates an air of expectancy and concentration on this strange sight. Tressel and Berkeley lead the way, followed by the corpse held shoulder-high and closely surrounded by the guards. Lady Anne follows in the rear. It is important to make clear to the audience that it is she alone who is responsible for this funeral rite of a dead king. The corpse is heavy, and the progress slow. The group of actors take their time in progressing across the stage. They give the audience time to both note the solemnity of the occasion, and also to register that the control and responsibility rests with the only woman on-stage: it is she who begins the spoken text with a command to, 'Set down, set down your honourable load.' As the body of Henry is referred to by Lady Anne throughout the scene, and indeed is used by her as her only defence against the onslaught of Richard's rhetoric, its position on-stage is important. The corpse ought to be physically, as it is metaphorically, central to the action of what follows. The actor playing the corpse is one of the silent characters, but throughout the scene he reminds the audience of what Richard has done in the very recent past, and of the nature of the occasion on which he has chosen to do his 'wooing'.

At Anne's command to set down the corpse, the bearers, guards, and Tressel and Berkeley, cease to have active roles to play in the proceedings and become passive spectators. They are an on-stage audience which begins to witness Anne's fulfilment of her role in this spectacle: the formal lamentation of 'virtuous Lancaster'. The presence of fifteen men gives this lament a public quality, and as a public act, a required performance, it carries with it the stress of responsibility for appropriate behaviour. Up to, and including this lament, Lady Anne is controlling the progress of the ritual, but immediately Richard enters the stage, this control is lost,

61

never to be regained. He takes over events, directs and manipulates them according to his own design. Even before he enters, the authority of Anne is undermined and she is seen as uncertain and tentative. She gives an order to go on, only to countermand it seconds later:

Come now, towards Chertsey with your holy load,
Taken from Paul's to be interreed there;
And still, as you are weary of this weight,
Rest you, whiles I lament King Henry's corse.
(lines 29–32)

Richard's entry is so well timed, coming as it does when the bearers are caught with the heavy corpse on their shoulders, uncertain whether to go on or stay, that he may well have been observing the events (visible to the audience perhaps) and waiting for his opportunity. When he intervenes, the bearers are not sure what to do. Anne has told them to take their 'holy load' up again and, even as they are doing so, orders them to 'rest'. Richard's opening line, 'Stay, you that bear the corse, and set it down', is spoken as if to intervene on Anne's behalf. It is as if Richard has taken over responsibility for the scene's ritual, and once this has demonstrably happened, Anne's control of events is critically weakened, just as her self-control will be undermined by Richard's actions. The formality of the funeral ritual, where all concerned know what to do and what to expect, instantly disappears with the arrival of Richard, and Lady Anne is denied the relative sense of security and comfort that comes from her participation in a scenario that is known and familiar. Those who, together with her, were a part of a ritual and had specific supporting roles to play (the fifteen men who accompany the corpse), are equally suddenly denied their role and their joint purpose is replaced by individual uncertainty about how to act. Instead of participants, they become observers. As such, their presence on-stage during the subsequent action reminds the audience in the theatre that collectively they have the physical power to intervene, but lack the will to do so.

Richard controls events through fear of what he might do, rather than through what he does, or even of what he is realistically capable of doing. What happens to Lady Anne is shocking, yet understandable, if seen in performance. It is akin to a nightmare in which a victim cries out for help, and although help is all around, it fails to materialize into action. Anne's seduction, or, as I prefer to think of it, her molestation by Richard, is witnessed by two equally helpless sets of spectators. Throughout the entire running time of this extraordinarily theatrical scene, only two lines are actually spoken by anyone other than Richard and Lady Anne, yet what they say, and its significance, can be understood by the reader only if he or she is prepared to recognize the role being played by the silent, but far from inconsequential characters on stage with them.

What I have suggested above in order to bring that scene to life is not, of course, *the* way to interpret what takes place, but it is *a* way of coming to terms with what to do with actors whom Shakespeare indicates are present, but does not clearly state why. My interpretation of this scene can quite easily be turned on its head. Let us suppose that the actress playing Lady Anne understands her character to be not someone weak and vulnerable, but a calculating mature woman who was never particularly close to her father-in-law and who is merely fulfilling a public duty which cannot be avoided. Furthermore, that actress may see Anne as shallow and power-hungry, and suppose her initial response to Richard to be only a sham because she is secretly pleased and flattered by the attentions of one so close to real political power. In this interpretation, Anne cannot behave other than as she does *because the presence of the other on-stage characters monitoring her speech and actions*, makes the occasion one in which it is necessary for her to present an appropriate public face. My point is that when you are reading, they, and other silent characters, cannot and should not be ignored. If they are there, then the reader must consciously make interpretative decisions as to what to do with them.

The potential significance of silent characters needs to be recognized by the active reader and their presence in the action of the performance text animated in the reader's imagination. But even characters who are given a good deal to say by a dramatist may still demand the creative invention of an actor to articulate moments when they have no words, but are still required to be articulate.

Janet Suzman, again returning to her role as Hedda Gabler in a production by Jonathan Miller, can help us here. She is speaking about times when Hedda is alone on stage, and wordless. Using the term 'silent soliloquy' to describe the opening of the second act, Suzman eloquently describes her enactment of the silent character. Ibsen gives the following stage direction:

The room at the Tesmans', as in the First Act, except that the piano has been taken away and a graceful little writing-table with a book-case put in its place. A smaller table has been put by the sofa on the left; most of the bouquets are gone, but Mrs Elvsted's stands on the large table in front of the stage. It is afternoon.

Hedda, in an afternoon dress, is alone in the room. She is standing by the open glass door, loading a pistol. The fellow to it lies in an open pistol-case on the writing-table.

From what Ibsen supplies in the printed text, Miss Suzman makes the following eloquent actor's text by using her creative imagination to manufacture meaning. I quote it at length because it seems to me to be precisely what should be looked for in an active reader's re-creation of an actor's text. Note her awareness of the significance of the environment for acting, of costume, properties and minor characters:

Ibsen describes in the stage directions merely Hedda's readiness to receive visitors, and she is busy loading the gun. So – the furniture is now moved to the disposition she prefers. Father's picture is by now in its place of honour on the wall of the inner room. Her old piano is likewise in that sanctum. The flowers are less profuse and more carefully placed ... the house is quiet. Tesman has gone out. Berta [the Tesman's servant] probably has her poor old exhausted feet up. Hedda has changed into an afternoon dress. A dull day. What will happen?

I thought perhaps I might not load the gun in full view. Gives the game away too soon. (I say game advisedly: Brack [a judge and friend of the Tesmans] knows her predilections of old.) If you are loading a gun it is pretty obvious that you will be using it sooner or later. And what about the piano? Why not play it? But she's too unsettled to sit down. So, I ran the butt of the gun down the keys. An ugly sound. Defiant. I wandered into the main room surveying the newly arranged furniture. It was better than it had been, but neither pleased me nor displeased me. I shoved the back of the rocking-chair as I passed. It rocked noisily on its own. Ghostly. I stood, unsure of what to do, toying with time. Time toying with me? The clock ticked. I remembered the gun in my hand and began polishing it with a piece of lint. What a splendid gleaming weapon. I loved it. I checked the sights and turned to take a mock-aim at something. Daddy's frozen glare caught my eye. I hated him. I nearly squeezed the trigger. Patricide!

Don't bother you fool – he's well and truly dead. Ah, but what does it feel like to kill *yourself*, I thought. I slowly brought the gun to my own temple, interested by the feel of cold metal on warm skin. It felt good to me, and strangely desirable. I must investigate whether this looks as ferocious and beautiful as I think. I went to the mirror above the desk to look, and posed in front of it – as an actress might, I fancied. A stray wisp of hair annoyed me. Spoiled the picture. I smoothed it into place, diverted from morbidity by vanity. I wished fleetingly I had hair like Thea's [Mrs Elvsted]. I heard the crackle of leaves from outside, and whirled round to see the Judge picking his way towards my house. The back way! How dare he, I thought. Too presumptuous by half. I shall give him a fright. So I did!

... for me this one-minute charade expanded her dilemma most explicitly. Emptiness, boredom, pistols, vanity, death and dying, time creeping past.[13]

Gesture

We have already seen that actors use more than the spoken word to compose their performance texts. Physical gesture is a very important part of our everyday body language, and actors use gesture in a significant way. Nodding at someone you know as you pass them in the street indicates recognition; raising your hat, waving, and so on, are all social gestures, signs which we make almost automatically. The language and vocabulary of gesture was more sophisticated and codified in Elizabethan England than it is now. The Shakespearean editor and scholar, David Bevington, reminds us that on the Elizabethan stage,

Kneeling, embracing, clasping of hands, bowing, removing the hat, assuming a proper place at table, deferring to others in going through a doorway – all are part of a rich vocabulary expressing contractual obligations, obedience, homage, submission, fealty, petition, hospitality, parental authority, royal prerogative.[14]

Bevington goes on to make the important point that

the very familiarity of such gesture generates also a language of nuance by means of which Elizabethan spectators might recognize, through subtle variations from the norm, signals of estrangement, defiance of authority, and other kinds of social inversion.[15]

Once the normative gestural response to, say, a greeting or farewell has been established in performance by the actors, its absence can be significant in a play from any period. However, perhaps one of the best examples to illustrate this point is the one chosen by Bevington himself, from *Richard II*.

Richard returns from a military campaign in Ireland to find Bolingbroke and his followers in revolt against the Crown. In Act III, Scene iii, outside the walls of Flint Castle, Bolingbroke is speaking throughout the entrance of Richard on to the walls of the castle. As Bolingbroke sees Richard, what the audience immediately notes is who, of those at stage level, kneel at the presence of the lawful king. Those who do (and there are some) and those who do not, are instantly registered and thus communicate to the audience the reality of the schism in the land. Their failure to observe the traditional form of public acknowledgement of the sovereign's power provides a powerful visual metaphor. The contradictory responses and the significance of the brief tableau is not lost on Richard:

RICHARD: We are amazed; and thus long have we stood
        To watch the fearful bending of thy knee,
        Because we thought ourself thy lawful king.

> And if we be, how dare thy joints forget
> To pay their awful duty to our presence?
> (lines 72–6)

You can see from that last quotation that the printed text itself contains the evidence required to establish the existence and significance in performance of a particular gesture.

Sometimes in the work of contemporary dramatists there is an extensive vocabulary of visual gesture made quite explicit by the stage directions. For example, in Samuel Beckett's *Waiting for Godot*, the enactment of Beckett's text requires the actors to be constantly aware of the need to make appropriate gestural language. Indeed, to give a faithful rendition of this text in performance, requires that the actors learn the words *and* the gestures that put those words in context. Look at the following brief extract from a speech by Pozzo in Act I. It is interesting and illustrative of the whole of the play in the amount of pantomimic action it requires in addition to specific gestures:

POZZO: Look. (*All look at the sky except Lucky who is dozing off again. Pozzo jerks the rope.*) Will you look at the sky, pig! (*Lucky looks at the sky.*) Good, that's enough. (*They stop looking at the sky.*) What is there so extraordinary about it? Qua sky? It is pale and luminous like any sky at this hour of the day. (*Pause.*) In these latitudes. (*Pause.*) When the weather is fine. (*Lyrical.*) An hour ago (*he looks at his watch, prosaic*) roughly (*lyrical*) after having poured forth ever since (*he hesitates, prosaic*) say ten o'clock in the morning (*lyrical*) tirelessly torrents of red and white light it begins to lose its effulgence, to grow pale (*gesture of the two hands lapsing by stages*) pale, ever a little paler, a little paler until (*dramatic pause, ample gesture of the two hands flung wide apart*) pppfff! finished! it comes to rest. But – (*hand raised in admonition*) – but behind this veil of gentleness and peace night is charging (*vibrantly*) and will burst upon us (*snaps his fingers*) pop! like that!

(Author's italics)

Minor Characters

In reading Shakespeare's plays, and in particular when reading the tragedies, it is possible to get caught up in an almost obsessive way with the fate of the great acting roles around which the text is built. As well as a host of silent characters, who are there in order to create a context in which the action of more eloquent characters is understood by an audience, there are many so-called 'minor' roles for actors. Such roles do not in themselves attract much attention in literary analysis, but may be of enormous significance when seen in performance. As a way of approaching a dramatist's text as an actor, go through the list of characters, and temporarily discard all those whose names you recognize. What you are left with may repay your study by deepening your understanding of how plays work. For example what are a Scottish Doctor and a Gentlewoman doing in the list of characters who appear in *Macbeth*? Let us look at these last two.

This pair actually appear together in one of the most famous scenes in all of Shakespeare: the sleepwalking scene (Act V, Scene i). If you are familiar with this scene, what you probably know about it is bound up with an image in your mind of Lady Macbeth, vulnerable, alone, and very close to death. But the scene opens with the presence on stage of the Doctor and Gentlewoman who wait for Lady Macbeth to enter. Their waiting, and what they have to say and do, prepares the audience for what they are about to witness. The audience learn that the two have waited before, and that Lady Macbeth has been seen to walk in her sleep. The enactment of sleepwalking is not a common occurrence on the Elizabethan or Jacobean stage, and Shakespeare uses the presence of these minor characters in part to ensure instant recognition of the signals given out by the actress playing Lady Macbeth for what they are intended to mean. For this reason, the opening fifteen lines of the scene begin that process of preparation. When the actress enters, she is immediately identified by the Gentlewoman (remember when Lady Macbeth was last seen she was wearing a costume which instantly identified her as a queen, and now she appears in a nightgown), 'Lo you! Here she comes. This is her very guise.' What the audience sees in the silent performance of the actress playing Lady Macbeth is verbally reinforced by the commentary, 'upon my life, fast asleep'. The Doctor and Gentlewoman then proceed to draw the attention of the audience to her hand in which she holds a lighted taper, a particularly potent and powerful symbol in this play. They ensure that the audience begins to grasp that its significance is more than practical: 'She has light by her *continually*' (author's italics). All the subsequent actions of Lady Macbeth in this, her last scene in the play, are commented upon by the Doctor and Gentlewoman in order that the audience is guided towards a recognition of the true significance of Lady Macbeth's silent actions. These two minor characters function as a chorus in this scene. They also have another major task: they help the audience to empathize with Lady Macbeth's self-inflicted hurt. Both characters are recognizable as caring – the Doctor for the health of the body, the Gentlewoman for the day-to-day needs of Lady Macbeth. Yet, despite being literally and symbolically close to her, neither can render any assistance or relief from

67

distress. Together, those minor characters introduce the important idea of the threat that exists to the mortal soul of Lady Macbeth. She is seen guarding a small light of conscience, but that light is extremely vulnerable and liable to go out at any moment. Her eventual suicide would have been seen by the original audience as a tragedy not least because suicide was believed to be a mortal sin, entailing the loss of eternal life. However, the audience have been prepared, and their comprehension of the action of the scene shaped, by the interjections and commentary provided by the Doctor and Gentlewoman. They speak of heaven, prayer, and God, and of the need for this confession (for confession is what Lady Macbeth's compulsive walking really is) to be heard by a priest, who can offer absolution and forgiveness, rather than by two people (and a whole theatre of others) who can offer only sympathy.

There are then no minor characters. You could argue that some are more marginal than others, but in Shakespeare in particular, that is an argument likely to lead you away from comprehending how the performance text works. In your study of his plays, and also those of other dramatists, never regard a character as superfluous, however little he or she may be given to say, or however infrequent his or her appearances on stage.

3 The Visual Text

A few years ago John Barton directed a production of *Richard II* for the RSC.[16] It was notable for two dominating ideas imposed by the director. Firstly, Barton made a casting decision to alternate the two leading actors in the roles of Richard and Bolingbroke. Secondly, he decided to stress what he saw as Richard's 'compulsive role-playing'. The designers for this show were Timothy O'Brien and Tazeena Firth. In an article about the collaboration, O'Brien wrote:

The designer had these thoughts in trying to present the play: first, there was the fact of the alternating leading players in the context of an acting company; secondly, there was the idea of Richard II as a compulsive role-player; thirdly, the sense that the play was like a bad dream with its central figures wandering without remedy towards certain destruction; and lastly, the great challenge of the play to a designer, the upper level at Flint Castle.[17]

You will note that the designer puts the director's *ideas* about the dramatist's text first, and gives them prominence over the *practical* problems posed by the text. The task of a modern theatre designer *is* to express ideas (usually those of the director) in visual terms. He or she has to create an appropriate and comprehensible language of symbols which will express the director's interpretation of the printed text in performance.

The Designer

The task that faces a theatre designer, or in our case, a reader attempting to construct a designer's visual text from a printed one, is principally to create an environment for acting, and in doing so to recognize that what is created is never neutral. From the minute that environment or 'setting' is seen by the audience, it will be transmitting signals to them; signals they may or may not be aware of receiving, but which none the less act, together with others generated in different but complementary ways (through words, gestures, costumes, properties, lighting and sound cues and so on) to manufacture meaning in the performance text. A designer's text is capable of articulating meaning as effectively as a printed or spoken one. Just as we try to 'read' people from their external appearance, so we also try to 'read' environments. A few minutes in the house of a new acquaintance, particularly if he or she is absent for long enough to let us take a good look round, will provide a host of information from which to make at least some preliminary judgements about his or her character and life-style. The fact that the signs may be misleading and contradictory does not stop the attempt to decipher them. Indeed, people either consciously or unconsciously furnish and decorate their homes to make statements about themselves. You might, for example, look to see if a house you are visiting for the first time has any books, and if so of what kind. Are there any pictures on the walls? Is the house tidy or untidy? Is it so clean as to make you feel uncomfortable? All these and many more impressions go to make up the 'feel' of the place. Obviously the impressions given by a particular environment may be misleading, and they may not have the same message for each interpreter, but they cannot be ignored: it is almost impossible entirely to divorce an individual from the setting in which they choose to be seen. Learning to read that setting or design involves consciously decoding the signals it gives out instead of simply being influenced by them subconsciously.

A clear example of an environment which is richly coded is provided by the carefully designed and controlled images presented to the television viewer in party political broadcasts. When party leaders or spokespersons are seen, great care has been taken to ensure that their immediate environment is appropriate to the image intended to be projected. Firstly, the setting itself is frequently illusionistic; it has been deliberately manufactured in every detail to look natural, spontaneous and 'real'. The viewer is never deliberately made aware of the presence of the special television lighting, the cameras, or the crew; and though the filming is usually done in a studio, what appears to be being shown is the speaker's own home or office. Within the last few years, designs deemed appropriate for the pronouncements of political leaders have usually included some of the following key elements. Almost always there are some books; the viewer cannot make out any titles, but they look weighty (literally), and are well-bound, and expensive – certainly not paperbacks! The books are there in the background as the part of the design which signals to the audience that their owner is both educated and has immediate access to information and knowledge. A carefully arranged vase of flowers may also be 'in-shot' for at least part of the broadcast. Flowers suggest a variety of meanings, among them the sensitivity of the leader to the natural world and to beauty. The arrangement of the flowers suggests a side to the personality which, while now exercising or seeking to exercise power on behalf of us all, has not lost touch with ordinary domestic life.

The architecture of the setting is also important and carries messages. Walls are often wood-panelled, suggesting permanence and antiquity.

Panelling also hints at a study, or an ancient seat of learning, thus lending to its (temporary) inhabitant an air of authority, permanence, and continuity with the past. The designer of all this also carefully selects furniture to make the required impression and to complement the other visual elements in the overall design. Almost certainly the final impression created will not be modern, nor will it appear over-elaborate or baroque. It will probably be comfortable, but not luxurious, and upholstered in delicate floral patterns or pastel shades. The whole environment will avoid extremes, will be clean, and very tidy; after all, it serves to represent an establishment that the designer wishes to convey exudes calm and order. The individual, or rather the group interest represented by that individual, at the centre and focus of this design, has a personal image which is equally carefully manufactured. Hair, clothes, posture, (seated figures are never placed well-back in the chair, but sit upright, ready to respond to any call immediately; the desired impression is of an alert rather than a relaxed stance); all the elements of personal presentation are carefully managed to get the right effect, as is the tone of the voice in which the spoken text will be delivered.

When you read a play as a director or actor, and certainly when you read it as a designer, it is very important to be able to locate the action taking place in the theatre of your mind's eye in a given playing- or theatre-space. From experience gained by theatre-going, you may decide to draw on your familiarity with a whole range of very different theatre spaces, ranging from small crowded and hot rooms over pubs, seating no more than fifty in varying degrees of discomfort, to huge air-conditioned auditoria seating upwards of two thousand. These very different kinds of spaces for acting establish particular performer–audience relationships, and may also create expectations about the theatrical conventions governing the staging of the play being watched. By no means all our theatres today comprise a proscenium-arch stage with fixed seating for the audience. At school or college you will probably already have encountered performances in a range of spaces, from purpose-built studios with flexible seating, to converted rooms, and over the floor of the school hall. Indeed, there is a growing awareness amongst performers and audiences alike, of the potential that exists for an exciting theatrical experience almost everywhere other than on the traditional proscenium-arch stage! You can, if you wish, use your imagination to create an ideal playing-space, or may choose to set the action in the light of what you know about the playing conditions for which the original performance material was designed. Although the task of a designer is to create an environment for acting, he or she has to do so within the limitations of the chosen performance space.

The Elizabethan and Jacobean Performance Space

Despite the vast amount of published literature, and the research that has been done on the playing conditions experienced by Elizabethan and Jacobean actors and audiences, hard facts are few in number, and there is much speculation. Several drawings exist (mostly from contemporary maps) of the exteriors of the public playhouses, but the only pictorial evidence of what the interiors may have looked like, and most importantly from our point of view, what the stage itself was like, comes to us from the De Witt drawing of the Swan playhouse. There are problems with the De Witt evidence: we do not know, for example, whether or not he was drawing a rehearsal or a performance. None the less, there are certain key features of the stage and auditorium which can be deduced from De Witt and other contemporary sources. For a detailed, but highly readable and authoritative account of the playing conditions of this period, consult Andrew Gurr's *The Shakespearean Stage, 1574–1642*.[18] For now let me simply set out the main features of the public theatres (of which the Swan was one) in order to assist you in recreating a visual text in that environment.

The theatres were open to the sky, although some of the audience was seated under cover, and the stage itself was partially shielded from the elements by a roof supported by two pillars which extended over it. The roof's underside was probably painted to represent the heavens. The stage was raised up both to improve the view, and to provide a very necessary area underneath it which could be exploited during the action. Projecting out into the body of the auditorium, the Elizabethan or Jacobean stage was surrounded on three sides by an audience of upwards of two thousand people. Its size, according to Gurr, was approximately equivalent to that of half a modern doubles-tennis court. At the rear of the stage, and forming a back wall visible to the audience, was the 'tiring' house. Here the actors waited for their entrances, and changed their costumes as the action dictated. Set into the façade were two large double doors. These doors provided the *only* opening for entrances and exits on to the stage. Above them, built into the façade, was a balcony.

Elizabethan public theatres made an excellent space for the actor. He was the focal point of interest (there were of course no women performers on the English professional stage until after the Restoration). The theatre space provided the actor with a very commanding position, and at the same time instilled such intimacy that he must have felt as if he were able to reach out and touch the audience. All worked together to get the groundlings, as a contemporary dramatist rather patronizingly put it,

On tiptoe, to reach up,
And (from rare silence) clap their brawney hands,
T'applaud what their charmed soul scarce understands.[19]

Of course there was little to distract the attention of the audience from the actor's craft or the language of the dramatist. Both actors and audience shared, as it were, the same space. They were not, as was to happen later, separated by a stage curtain, or by artificial light; neither was the stage full of elaborate or spectacular scenery.

There was another kind of theatre-space being used at this time: the so-called private theatre. The main difference, as far as we are concerned, is really one of scale. Private theatre performances took place indoors in much smaller auditoria. Often plays for private theatres were performed at night; the lighting for the stage, and that for the auditorium, was from the same source. It was more expensive to go to the private theatres; therefore the audience was less mixed than at, say, the Globe or the Swan. Although they were used by the adult players, and by troupes of boy players who never, as far as is known, ventured on to the public stage, the repertoire of both kinds of theatres was essentially interchangeable.

When attempting to animate a visual text for a play of this period, whether it was first written for the public or the private theatre is not really significant. What is important is that both spaces had three distinct areas for playing: the main stage itself, the area under that stage, and a raised area or balcony, and that there were two entrances/exits on to the main stage set into the back wall. Both spaces used a theatrical convention that we now term *non-representational*.

When you sit down to read Shakespeare, Marlowe, Webster or any other dramatist of this period, you will not find in their printed texts a detailed description of how the playwright envisaged the physical location or setting for the action. Indeed, sometimes you may have to look very hard at what is being said and implied by the spoken text in order to begin to imagine the setting for yourself. Their theatrical convention allowed for the physical and geographical location of a scene to be established through the dialogue spoken by the actors:

VIOLA: What Country, friends, is this?
CAPTAIN: This is Ilyria, Lady.
          (*Twelfth Night*, I, ii, lines 1–2)

Of course this is not to suggest that the stage of the public theatre or that of the private was clothed only by the imagination thus cued by the actors. It may well have been the practice of Elizabethan players to indicate a specific location not only through the language, but also by using a simply built stage-construction such as a tree made out of canvas and wood that could stand to represent, say, the Forest of Arden. Unlike later nineteenth-century conventions of *representational* or *illusionistic* staging, the 'tree' would be on-stage to *represent* reality, rather than attempting, at any level, to encourage the audience in the belief that it *was* the thing it represented. The reality of a setting of a play by Shakespeare is, essentially, an imaginative one, created and sustained by the collective collaboration of the audience's imagination. The famous chorus at the beginning of Shakespeare's *Henry V* reminds us that it is on the forces of the audience's imagination that the verisimilitude depends:

CHORUS: ... let us ...
> *On your imaginary forces work.*
> *Suppose* within the girdle of these walls
> Are now confined two mighty monarchies,
> Whose high uprearèd and abutting fronts
> The perilous narrow ocean parts asunder:
> *Piece out our imperfections with your thoughts.*
> Into a thousand parts divide one man,
> And make imaginary puissance:
> *Think, when we talk of horses, that you see them*
> Printing their proud hoofs i' th' receiving earth;
> For *'tis your thoughts that now must deck our kings,*
> Carry them here and there, jumping o'er times,
> Turning the accomplishment of many years
> Into an hour-glass ...

(Author's italics)

Where the action of the play took place was of significance to Shakespeare, and to his audience. The plays are, after all, set in extraordinarily diverse locations: ancient Greece and Rome, Cyprus and Denmark, Venice and Verona, a tropical island. But it is the atmospheric qualities of that location, and the nature of the people who inhabit it as revealed by what they say and do during the performance itself, that counts; not the physical attempt to portray on stage what it might or might not have looked like geographically or architecturally.

The Nineteenth-Century Theatre Space

Representational staging, that is the presentation on the stage of a total environment for acting, complete, and designed to the last detail, only became physically possible to stage convincingly (that is illusionistically) in the nineteenth century. Technological innovations, and the architecture of the nineteenth-century theatres themselves, facilitated illusion. Audiences were encouraged in their willing suspension of disbelief to accept that what they were observing with their eyes and ears *was* real. Think for a minute of the way in which the shipwreck at the beginning of Shakespeare's *The Tempest* is written. Note how it relies on the power of the language and the skill of the actors to enact it successfully. Now compare the way in which you can deduce it would originally have been staged with a nineteenth-century version of a shipwreck, staged in London in 1852, and reported in the *Illustrated London News*:

The tossing and rolling of the vessel amid the tumult and the darkness, made visible by the lightning flash, was managed with a reality that brought at once sea, sky and storm-tossed bark not only before the imagination, but the vision. Then the sudden going down of the ship! It was terrible. The horrified shriek of the audience almost substituted that of the crew.[20]

At the start of a play performed on the Victorian stage, the lights in the auditorium would be dimmed (a nineteenth-century innovation) and the curtain raised to reveal a stage picture framed by the elaborately decorated arch of the proscenium. The proscenium arch signalled, as did the separate lighting of the stage and auditorium, the absolute separation, by an imaginary fourth wall, of the world of the stage and that of the auditorium. Actors and audiences no longer shared the same space, nor did they enjoy the same immediacy of contact as their Elizabethan predecessors. The separation needed to be insisted upon, for if the actors had acknowledged the presence of the audience and hence the fact that they were 'acting', then the illusion that sustained their separate identities as the characters they played would have been broken.

The nineteenth-century theatre in Britain produced a great deal of spectacular theatre. In many ways it must often have seemed a theatre dominated by the appeal to the eye over that of the ear. Certainly many potential dramatists were not content to have their work used merely as a vehicle for spectacular effects, and chose rather to write novels. However, in Europe, if not immediately in Britain, the new ability to create realistic stage settings was put to effective dramatic use in an alliance with the spoken word to manufacture meaning in the play in performance. For an excellent example of the expressive power of the visual text made possible by developments in nineteenth-century theatre, I want to turn to a play of the nineteenth century which presupposes the use in performance of a representational setting.

The Norwegian dramatist Henrik Ibsen was well aware of the potential power of the carefully contrived visual image to convey meaning in the theatre. In his text *A Doll's House* (1879), he takes great pains to be specific about the environment which his principal characters, Helmer and Nora, have created for themselves. Of course he does so not only because he knows the theatre is capable of realistically representing his design, but also because he is writing a particular kind of play. *A Doll's House* is a *naturalistic* drama: a play which seeks, like the then-contemporary scientific inquiry into the behaviour of the animal species, to investigate and record the human condition through a careful and detailed observation of human activity in its given environment. To see and observe the humans in their self-made environment was crucial to successful and accurate observation. To see and to understand *where* they live, is to begin to see and understand *how* they live. The whole of the action of *A Doll's House* takes place in one room. That room is given the following description by Ibsen in his stage directions, directions that articulate a fascinating visual text:

A pleasant room, tastefully but not expensively furnished. On the back wall, one door to the right leads to the entrance hall, a second door on the left leads to HELMER's study. Between these two doors, a piano. In the middle of the left wall, a door; and downstage from it, a window. Near the window a round table with armchairs and a small sofa. In the right wall, upstage, a door; and on the same wall downstage, a porcelain stove with a couple of armchairs and a rocking-chair. Between the stove and the door a small table. Etchings on the walls. A what-not with china and other small objets d'art; a small book-case with books in handsome bindings. Carpet on the floor; a fire burns in the stove.

The stage directions which follow on from this description make it clear that Ibsen wanted the audience in the theatre to be given time to take in this design before the arrival of any of the characters. We hear Nora before we see her. How then can *we* read this visual text? It would appear that the inhabitants of this room are not wealthy, but they have used what money they do have to buy furniture that reflects their upwardly mobile social aspirations. They have a piano, not of course unusual in any nineteenth-century European household, but as well as being a means of entertainment a piano also hints at artistic sensibility. There are engravings on the walls because the couple cannot afford original paintings (nor would they know what to buy), yet feel the need to display the fact that they are, in however small a way, patrons of the arts. The bookcase is small and full of expensively bound volumes, thus making complete a series of messages which are meant to indicate to the observer or observant reader that this couple is cultured because committed to all the arts: music, art and literature. However, the piano, etchings and books have a decorative rather than a functional appearance. The focal point of the room is the traditional Norwegian porcelain stove. Attention is drawn to the stove because it is lit, and also through the information that it is surrounded by two armchairs and a rocking-chair: the latter in particular is a symbol of simple domesticity and comfort. The responsibility for the arrangement of the room is Torvald's. Nora remarks that 'Torvald has certainly the art of making a home bright and beautiful.' However, the what-not is obviously Nora's. It is filled with small objects, insignificant in themselves, collected by her. These add up to a suggestion that she may be preoccupied with, and certainly hoards, trivia (a verbal clue to her nature is provided by Torvald who frequently refers to her as his 'little squirrel'). Everything in this room appears to have its own carefully allotted place; it has been arranged to look at its best and suggests a doll's house arranged by an adult, not a child.

You don't even have to read *A Doll's House* before you get a distinctly strong impression from that opening description by Ibsen of the visual text (the environment for acting that he envisaged) of what the characters who made it for themselves to inhabit are going to be like. The messages being transmitted to the audience by that design idea are important, and need to be recognized and decoded if the transition from text into performance is to be effected. But the messages given in the printed text are incomplete. Ibsen provides an outline, but the details remain to be completed. For example, he makes no mention of what would be an appropriate choice of colours. What kind of piano is it? Are there little 'bits and pieces' left lying casually around the room (newspapers, a book or magazine, a piece of clothing), or is everything carefully in place and neatly arranged? Your decisions on what to include or exclude from this visual text are based on what Ibsen gives as a starting point, but you can only begin to make decisions when you have settled on the kind of image you want to create and why. Its appropriateness will be judged by the extent to which it serves the ideas and mood of the printed text. As I read it, the visual text of *A Doll's House* should communicate the couple's preoccupation with the material world: this room, and the things within it, give an outward impression of order, calm and ordinariness. Nothing in the environment gives offence; nothing stands out. It all blends together in a kind of social and domestic camouflage, concealing for the time being the chaos of the inner lives of Nora and Torvald. As the play unfolds, the tensions emerge until action is eventually brought to a halt by the sound of a heavy door being slammed shut (a signal of defiance not only to Torvald but also to the neighbours!), as Nora breaks free of the life and the environment which has changed from what at first seemed

77

to be acceptably warm and cosy, to being recognizably stultifying and oppressive.

Ibsen, and other nineteenth-century dramatists, who wrote for a representational illusionistic theatre, are able to give the reader a clear picture of the kind of visual environment in which action is to be played out. None the less, *A Doll's House* still leaves a designer, or a reader, fastidious in his or her respect for the playwright's intentions, a great deal of scope for interpretative decisions. To be faithful to what a dramatist intended it is not necessary slavishly to follow his or her directions to the letter, even supposing the means to do so are available. Today audiences, readers and playwrights are familiar with both representational and non-representational settings, and thus when you take on the creative task of making an appropriate visual text for *A Doll's House* you may legitimately express Ibsen's ideas in completely abstract visual terms. You can reject the representational convention altogether, but you must not reject the meanings which it was originally there to represent. No matter how you decide to approach the design problems inherent in the creation of any performance text, you must find a way of visually representing the central ideas and feelings that have emerged as a result of your close study of the printed text. To undertake that thinking process adequately and appropriately, you must be able to 'read' the playwright's design, even if you subsequently decide to modify, or even reject it. You certainly cannot begin to understand what the characters *say* in *A Doll's House* (or indeed in any other nineteenth-century naturalistic drama) unless you can read the visual *context* in which it is said.

A recent production of *A Doll's House* by the RSC can, I think, show us something of how a contemporary designer constructs a visual text in relation to modern playing conditions and conventions whilst remaining true to Ibsen. This particular production was first staged at the Other Place in Stratford. It later transferred to the Pit, the studio-theatre in the RSC's London home at the Barbican. Both spaces are small, seating less than 200 people, with the audience in close proximity to the acting area. Each is adequately but basically equipped. The audience in both usually sits on three sides of the acting area.

The design budget for the production was small in comparison to that available for shows in the main house. The designer, Kit Surrey, could not, even if he had wished to, create a three-dimensional setting complete with walls and ceiling. He had not the money, the space, or the inclination. A replica of Ibsen's visual text could not be reproduced. Together with the director of the production, Kit Surrey nevertheless managed to maintain fidelity to the dramatist's text. He distilled what he thought to be significant in what Ibsen had said, and made a design on the basis of it that suited the playing conditions of the studio theatres. Kit Surrey designed a carpet. It was brown and thick, the kind of floor-covering that muffles sound by absorbing noises, particularly those of footsteps. It was cut in such a way as to draw attention to something which almost goes unnoticed in Ibsen's design: the number of entrances and exits in this room. The carpet emphasized the doors and gave the set a feeling of being surrounded by other rooms – not only in the apartment itself, but also in the rest of the building. Privacy in this environment is at a premium. Kit Surrey thus rightly stressed the fact that Nora and Torvald live in an apartment, not a detached house. The couple take great pains not to disturb their neighbours, and manifest an acute awareness of the possibility that they might be overheard. They protect their public image, and like so very many others, do so by trying never to give cause for remark, let alone for complaint.

On this brown carpet, Kit Surrey placed furniture and effects carefully chosen to signal the status and image that this couple wish to present to the world and to themselves. Everything the audience can see has been deliberately placed there; nothing is accidental. Colours, shapes, the design of the furniture, and the way in which it has been made, the interior fittings, all these and more add up to a modern visual text that establishes a mood, atmosphere and appropriate environment in which actors speak this nineteenth-century dramatist's text.

We are today familiar with a great variety of playing-spaces, and we produce dramatists, actors, designers and directors who are able to work within representational and non-representational conventions. For example, our National Theatre is in fact three theatres: the largest, the Olivier, has a large thrust-stage facing steeply banked rows of fixed seating. It is a design based on a classical Greek theatre at Epidaurus. The second space in the complex, the Lyttleton, is smaller than the Olivier, and has a conventional proscenium-arch stage. It too has fixed seating. The smallest playing space in the building, the Cottesloe, is the most flexible of all. It is a studio theatre, basically a box which can be adapted and changed to suit whatever actor–audience relationship may be required by the director working with the designer. In all these spaces, you can, if you wish, reproduce the playing conditions and actor–audience relationship of almost any period in theatre history.

Costume

A designer's text consists not only of an environment for acting, but also of what it has been decided is appropriate for the actors to wear. Costume

79

generates a whole series of signs and signals in the performance text, and playwrights, designers, and you as an active reader, must be aware of its potential power to make meaning. In our day-to-day lives, clothes, and the way they are worn, are highly significant. They are part of the way in which consciously or unconsciously we express our personality and status, and, to some extent, what we wear will produce, at least initially, both positive and negative reactions in those we meet.

Costumes worn by actors and actresses in a performance text are often used to locate the action on stage both historically and geographically. Costume can also be used as part of the visual text highlighting differences in social class and status; or signifying outwardly an inner change in the character wearing it. Costume can create splendid visual stage pictures, and can also isolate an individual actor from a host of others. Designers of costume can help in the manufacture of an effective performance and can also assist the performances of individual actors and actresses by subtly encouraging the audience to focus its attention in specific ways. For example, in a production of Shakespeare's *Henry VIII* at Stratford in 1983, the designer, Deirdre Clancy, used colour in her costumes in key areas (on caps, bodices, cuffs) in order to concentrate the attention of the audience on the eyes, faces and hands of the cast.

Dramatists often have characters draw attention to what they are wearing. Look, for example, at the following exchange between two female characters in Thomas Dekker's *The Shoemaker's Holiday* (1599):

ROSE: Get thee to London, and learn perfectly
Whether my Lacy go to France or no:
Do this, and I will give thee for thy pains
My cambric apron, and my Romish gloves,
My purple stockings, and a stomacher.
Say, wilt thou do this, Sybil, for my sake?

SYBIL:

Will I, quoth a? At whose suit? By my troth, yes, I'll go: a cambric apron, gloves, a pair of purple stockings, and a stomacher! I'll sweat in purple, mistress, for you; I'll take anything that comes, a God's name! O rich, a cambric apron!

(I, iii, lines 52–62)

The significance of that exchange, where a woman of higher social status offers her clothes to one of a lower social group, would have been magnified for an Elizabethan audience because of their familiarity with the elaborate contemporary dress code which was actually enshrined in law (although, as the text itself seems to suggest, the extent to which the dress code was enforced is uncertain). We do know that certain kinds of material were, nominally at least, reserved for particular social groups, a practice that continued into the nineteenth century. In our own society different social groups are often recognizable through what they wear: punks, Sloane rangers, rockers and so on, all have an elaborate but almost immediately recognizable dress code. But the Elizabethan code was perhaps even more elaborate and complex, and extended to colours as well as to materials and the way in which they were worn. Despite this, the signs they emitted could readily be decoded on the stage and in the street.

In the theatre, costumes were certainly a vital ingredient in making successful performances. They were also, aside from his voice, an actor's most precious and valuable possession. Costumes worn by actors were sometimes bequeathed, or purchased at great expense from the nobility and were tailored from fine materials, generally unavailable to most people even if they could afford to buy them. The inventory of one of the Elizabethan player's companies (Henslowe's) gives a vivid description of the kind of garments that were to be seen on the Elizabethan stage:

1 A scarlett cloke wth brode gould Laces: w^t gould buttons of the sam downe the sids

2 ... A scarlett cloke Layd downe w^t silver Lace and silver buttens ...[21]

The costumes were worn without very much regard to as either period or historical accuracy. Leading players had their own wardrobes from which they selected as they saw fit. The company wardrobe was used by the hired men and contained, according to Michael Hattaway, costumes that could be 'read' by an audience in the following way:

characters of high degree wore robes with heraldic or ecclesiastical emblems ... doctors' gowns were of scarlet, lawyers' gowns of black, rustics and clowns wore 'startups' (boots that reached to mid-calf), allowed fools wore long coats of motley woven of coarse wool and part coloured green and yellow ... virgins wore white, prologues wore black ... shepherds wore white coats and carried staff and bottle, sailors wore canvas suits, servants bluecoats or slops.[22]

A stage bedecked with kings and queens, lords and ladies, the great, if not the good, must indeed have been a spectacular sight, if only for the contrast between the clothes worn by most of the audience, and those sported by the actors. The wearing of costume technically belonging to the aristocracy was not unproblematic. Actors themselves were men of humble origins. Clothed as they often were, they seemed to some to be claiming or affecting a status to which they had no legitimate claim. In *Tudor Drama and Politics*, David Bevington shows how this tension between players and the power they imitated was effectively used to make political observations. No wonder the Puritans so vehemently objected to the players who not only flouted the rules of conduct that sustained the social order, but did so with apparent impunity and before others who might choose to follow their example:

In Stage Playes for a boy to put on the attyre, the gesture, the passions of a woman; for a meane person to take upon the title of a Prince with counterfeit porte, and traine, is by outward signs to show themselves otherwise than they are, and so within the compasse of a lye ... We are commanded by God to abide in the same calling wherein we were called, which is our ordinary vocation in a commonweale ... If privat men be suffered to forsake theire calling because they desire to walke gentlemen-like in sattine and velvet, with a bucler at their heeles, proportion is so broken, unitie dissolved, harmony confounded, that the whole body must be dismembered and the prince or the head cannot chuse but sicken.[23]

But costume on the Elizabethan stage was worn not simply to amaze and astonish the groundlings, or to deliberately antagonize the Puritans. It could be, and was used in a very sophisticated way as part of the visual text. In *Action is Eloquence*, Bevington cites the following example of how costume can be used to make meaning:

King Lear's journey from regal autocracy through madness to tearful reconciliation with Cordelia is signalled at every crucial turning by what he wears, by his royal robes, by his running 'unbonneted' in the storm, by the 'lendings' at which he tears and the weeds with which he is madly bedecked, by the 'fresh garments' suited to his royal rank in which he is vested at Cordelia's behest.[24]

It is not only Shakespeare and Elizabethan and Jacobean dramatists who are dramatically conscious of the potential of costume for effective theatre language. In Brecht's *Mother Courage* the playwright demonstrates an acute awareness of the power of the visual image created through costume, and with extreme economy achieves a memorable effect through contrasting two colours: red and black. The camp whore Yvette Pottier, is first seen by the audience in scene three, sewing at a coloured hat. She is described by Brecht in his stage directions as 'a very good-looking young person'. She owns a pair of red boots, and these are placed close by her. In productions I have seen of this play (most recently by the RSC at the Barbican with Judi Dench as Mother Courage), the boots and the hat make, literally, a splash of colour in an otherwise drab world. The red is a gay colour, entirely appropriate to one so young and full of life (Kattrin, Mother Courage's daughter, puts on the garments with delight when her mother's back is turned, only to be greeted with a searing rebuke). Kattrin is chastised because Mother Courage knows what the boots signify: they are the tools of Yvette's trade. They are used to attract clients, for Yvette, in common with others of her class, is forced to sell her body in order to survive.

Black is the other colour associated with Yvette. It is used to illustrate the cost to her of what she is forced to sell. In an off-stage action, Yvette marries a rich elderly officer. Towards the end of the play (in scene eight) she returns. The image of the young and beautiful girl is replaced by a new image. (In the Berlin production Brecht recalled that the actress playing Yvette padded her costume until she looked like a small barrel, walked with the aid of a stick, and had powdered her face heavily.) She is now dressed entirely in black. The black dress is a garment of mourning for her dead husband, but the mourning is only a sham as far as Yvette is concerned. She tells Mother Courage that she wears it because it suits her; indeed it does suit her, but not in the way she imagines. Yvette's consciousness cannot see what the audience see if they have made the connections in the text that Brecht hoped for. Yvette is in black because it represents the death of her youth, the death of her promise, the death of her physical health. Her wealth has been bought at usurious interest, and we should mourn her lost self.

Perhaps the best and most famous example of the potential of costume to make eloquent statements in performance is provided by Hamlet. Shakespeare is careful and deliberate when he specifies his hero's 'inky cloak' and 'customary suits of solemn black' (Act I, Scene ii, lines 77–8). Of course while this costume serves as an outward display of Hamlet's state of mourning for the death of his father, it could be identified in the mind of the audience as appropriate garb for one suffering from the fashionable disease of melancholia. But it also operates emblematically, to signal what is to come. Hamlet will need these funeral clothes for the deaths of Ophelia, Polonius, Laertes and his mother, it is indeed too early for him to '... cast thy nighted colour off' (Act I, Scene ii, line 68) as his mother bids him. Hamlet will be dressed throughout the play ready for his own funeral.

On a practical rather than a symbolic level, Hamlet's costume isolates him visually from all the other characters on-stage with whom he appears; it continually draws the attention of the audience on to him. This simple but effective costume works to very good effect from the very first time the audience are allowed to catch sight of Hamlet. In the first scene of the play, the audience see the ghost of his father and know, before the Prince himself, that something is indeed 'rotten in the state of Denmark.' (Act I, Scene iv, line 90). But what is wrong, and why, remains as much of a mystery to them as to Horatio and the other on-stage witnesses of the extraordinary events in that famous opening scene. What the audience *do* know is that the apparition, dumb to Horatio, *will* speak to Hamlet. His name is presented to the audience at the end of scene one as belonging to the man who will be the key to unlock the answers to the questions posed: Hamlet is the detective who, the audience hopes, will be capable of unravelling the clues satisfactorily. At the beginning of scene two his appearance immediately enables that audience to put a face to the name they already know and expect so much from.

Hamlet's entrance on to the playing area is thus carefully prepared by Shakespeare. Scene two opens with a procession on to the stage. It is a formal entrance of a large group of players, all of whom are being seen as their characters by the audience for the first time. In the procession are Claudius, Gertrude, Polonius, Laertes, Voltimand, Cornelius and Councillors, Attendants and Hamlet himself. The entrance on to the stage heralds a state occasion, and one that in this case begins with important and pressing political business. The audience see Claudius exercising his recently acquired power. Both he, and his queen, Gertrude, need to be immediately recognized by the audience in accordance with their status. Costume would, of course, be the obvious way of doing this. Theoretically, the scene ought to be dominated by the presence of the King, demonstrably in control of events, and giving orders for the direction of the state with calm authority and assurance. What Claudius has to *say* does seem to do this. His speeches monopolize the scene and verbally claim it as his (he speaks virtually the whole of the opening forty-nine lines). And yet, Claudius is prevented from dominating the action in the performance text by the brooding, silent, but highly visible figure in the 'inky cloak', Hamlet. Because of this visual counterpoint to what would otherwise be a scene dominated by the figure of Claudius, it is not surprising that the first lines Hamlet speaks are not delivered to any characters on-stage, but are addressed to the audience. In a sense, in performance, theirs is a special relationship. Shakespeare has ensured that expectations are aroused and focused on the subsequent performance of the prince.

As we have seen, in plays by Shakespeare (and his contemporaries) clothes worn by actors on stage in performance are never simply a means of self-advertisement and display. They can be used (as in *King Lear*) to express the changing inner state of a character's mind, and costume in *Hamlet* is seen to tell the audience something about the character's state of mind, his relationship to those around him, and also to prepare the audience for events to come. An even more powerful and complex use of costume to make significant textual statements is at work in *Macbeth*.

In Act III, Scene iv, a banquet has been prepared for Macbeth. The meal is a significant public and state occasion for the new king and his queen. It is an opportunity for both to display and enjoy in public the outward signs of their newly and bloodily acquired status and power. To do this they employ the conventional and expected signs: royal jewels and their emblems of state. Lady Macbeth is the hostess at what ought to be, for her and for her husband, a triumphant celebration and affirmation of all they have struggled to achieve. It is, I suggest, particularly important in the performance text you are preparing to see that what Lady Macbeth wears at this, her first state banquet, reflects and emphasizes her new social and political status, and the corresponding gain in both material power and wealth. As we know, the banquet is a disaster, not a triumph. The public display by the king and queen is undermined and exposed by the appearance to Macbeth of Banquo's ghost. The outward display of regal behaviour by Macbeth is stripped away, and his public mask replaced by his private face of terror. The effect in performance of the stripping away of a façade is helped if Macbeth's costume, like that of his wife, is one that emphasizes temporal power and dignity. Those robes that signify his high office and the respect due to it, are, on Banquo's appearance, made to seem ill-fitting and inappropriate.

If Lady Macbeth has also been shown in this scene in the costume of a powerful queen, one intent upon impressing others with the legitimacy of her new status, then so much the greater will be the shock to the audience of the contrast between that image and what is seen on the next occasion when Lady Macbeth enters the stage. Then, in Act V, Scene i, the famous sleep-walking scene, she appears stripped of the outward signs, symbols and show of state power for which she was prepared to risk anything and sacrifice anybody. Now the audience see her not as a public figure, but as a private individual behind the official public face. This change is emphasized by her altered costume; Shakespeare is careful to specify that she is to appear in her nightgown.

After the murder of Duncan, those characters who are awakened are also presumably seen to enter the stage in their nightgowns, for they are subsequently told to 'put on manly readiness' (line 130). We can assume the murdered king was killed in his nightgown. Hence, through costume there is a visual link established for the audience between the appearance of Lady Macbeth and the shared guilt of regicide. The actual costume worn by the actress is not necessarily, of course, a flimsy piece of material barely concealing her body. But it is a significant direction by Shakespeare because it is a garment worn in the privacy of the bedchamber, simple and unadorned, and certainly not designed for public display. Yet this scene *is* public. Lady Macbeth appears under the watching eyes of those two minor (but for this scene significant) characters: the Doctor and the

Gentlewoman. Their presence, and Lady Macbeth's appearance in her nightgown, is Shakespeare's way of making clear to the audience in the theatre her new vulnerability, and her exposure both to herself and to others. The nightgown symbolizes the stripping-away of the public outer shell to reveal what has happened to the woman beneath it. The change in Lady Macbeth from the confident and assertive queen, to desperate, pitiful and isolated woman, registers on the collective mind of the audience because, in part, that change is expressed in the visual text through costume.

I will return again to this interesting scene in due course, for it has much to teach us about how to transform a printed text into a performance. Before leaving the subject of costume, it should be noted that it is not by any means always necessary to imagine its use in the detail set out here. For example, Trevor Nunn's 1976 production of *Macbeth* for the Royal Shakespeare Company (designed by John Napier) opened up an interesting range of possible interpretations through the use of costume. Each player, from Ian McKellen (as Macbeth) to Judi Dench (as Lady Macbeth), wore whatever seemed to the designer appropriate to his or her character regardless of any historical or period consistency. The costumes eventually worn in performance at the Other Place, and later in a televised performance, were a deliberate mixture of styles and periods. It was therefore impossible for the audience to use costume to locate the play in any one particular historical period. The point the director and designer were using costume to make was that *Macbeth* is not an historical play, or a play in which the action is set in a time long-distant where people believed in witchcraft, but a play in which the characters are enmeshed in evil – and evil is timeless.

In the previous chapter on the performer's text, I suggested that our current theatre practice is dominated by the director. There are those who argue however, that the supremacy of the director in the creative process has been overtaken by the designer. It is certainly true that, in recent years, we have seen a return to more elaborate settings in productions of classic plays. Design now seems more and more a significant, some would say obtrusive, part of our experience of watching a play in performance. Whatever you think about the current fashions for presenting the visual text in performance, do remember that your task is to activate your imaginary forces as prompted by the cues in the printed text, in order to *see* the characters at work in your imagined environment, manufacturing text-into-performance.

4 Theatrical Ephemera?

WEIGEL'S PROPS

Just as the millet farmer picks out for his trial plot
The heaviest seeds and the poet
The exact words for his verse so
She selects the objects to accompany
Her characters across the stage. The pewter spoon
Which Courage sticks
In the lapel of her Mongolian jacket, the party card
For warm-hearted Vlassova and the fishing net
For the other, Spanish mother or the bronze bowl
For dust-gathering Antigone. Impossible to confuse
The split bag which the working woman carries
For her son's leaflets, with the moneybag
Of the keen tradeswoman. Each item
In her stock is hand-picked: straps and belts
Pewter boxes and ammunition pouches; hand-picked too
The chicken and the stick which at the end
The old woman twists through the draw-rope
The Basque woman's board on which she bakes her bread
And the Greek woman's board of shame, strapped to her back
With holes for her hands to stick through, the Russian's
Jar of lard, so small in the policeman's hand; all
Selected for age, function and beauty
By the eyes of the knowing
The hands of the bread-baking, net-weaving
Soup-cooking connoisseur
Of reality.

(From *Bertolt Brecht Poems*)[25]

Stage Properties

The Peter Hall diaries provide a mine not just of good gossip, but some fascinating material about the process of text-into-performance in our contemporary theatre. At one point Hall gives a first-hand account of the effect of properties on actors in rehearsal:

We rehearsed the *Hamlet* graveyard scene this morning with a real skull. The actuality of the scene was immediately apparent; actors, stage management, everybody aware of a dead man's skull among us.[26]

Properties then, may inspire and stimulate the work of a group of players. They also can, as Hall's writing reveals, point up practical problems of staging of which the reader is all too often totally unaware. Of that same scene, Hall identifies a series of problems:

Where can you keep the spade? Where can you put the coffin? How does Laertes get in and out? How do the grave diggers get in and out?[27]

But when the practicalities have been satisfactorily resolved, then the focus can turn to the significance of properties in the performance text.

Many now-distinguished actors have begun their careers as spear-carriers in productions of classic plays in the English repertoire. It is lowly but dignified work, and, as we have seen, not without the potential for creating significance in an overall performance text. With or without his spear, the silent actor is always signifying something to an audience whenever he is on-stage. What I want us to look at now however, is not the actor, but his spear! Stage properties, and their potential contribution to a play's meaning in performance, are very often passed over by the reader, but they are almost always significant objects. You must take note when a dramatist specifies the use of a specific prop, and then decide imaginatively how it is to be employed in the action and why. Props help create mood and atmosphere; they can create locale, and they are an aid to actors in the creation of a performance text. The right choice of property can, as I will try to illustrate, actually impose, or at least reinforce, a specific directorial interpretation of a scene.

It is helpful to distinguish, as they do in the theatre, between movable stage properties, such as beds, chairs, benches, candlesticks, vases of flowers and so on, and personal props, that is, those used in performance by an actor and actually carried by him, or at least used by him exclusively in the action. They include such things as rings, watches, matches, cigarette lighters, keys and so on. The first category is particularly able to contribute to meaning in Shakespeare and other Elizabethan or Jacobean dramatists. For example:

Beds in Shakespeare are . . . apt to juxtapose innocence with intrusion and violation. The bed's traditional associations of peace and intimacy are invoked as a backdrop to violence and death [the murder of Desdemona by Othello actually on their marriage-bed is an obvious example of this] much as the throne serves to put spectators in mind of a majesty that is often desecrated.[28] [The use of the throne is particularly significant in *Richard II*.]

As we have already seen in the chapter on the visual text, nineteenth-century dramatists were very much alive to the potential dramatic sig-

nificance in performance of both movable and non-movable stage properties. Ibsen's use of the books, piano, etchings and so on, in the setting he
envisaged for the enactment of *A Doll's House* is a clear example. Both
stage and personal properties can trigger associations for an audience. In
Chekhov's *The Cherry Orchard*, Lopakhin, the self-made man, is someone
who is continually aware, to the point of obsession, with the passing of
time. Almost his first words, and those of the play itself, concern its
passing: 'The train's arrived, thank God. What time is it?' Having a
pocket-watch as a personal prop (Chekhov's dialogue reveals that he
looks at his watch at least three times in Act I) will help the actor playing
the role to focus the attention of the audience on to this relatively small,
but in the context of the events of the play as a whole, significant detail of
the action. For Lopakhin is a man of, as far as the Ranyevskaia family
are concerned, tomorrow's world: a world rapidly encroaching on to their
estate, a world of modern communications, like the train and the telegraph,
in which a concern for time predominates. Liubov Andryeevna, in particular, appears always to seek to travel back in time (perhaps to her nursery
where the action of the play begins), and the text suggests that other
characters experience a distortion in time living either in the past, or in
some imaginary future. Only Lopakhin, it seems, is connected to, and
lives in and for, the present. His watch reminds him, and the audience, of
the fact of time passing.

I recall another personal property specified by Chekhov and emphasized
in a Peter Gill production of this play. The actress playing Varia carried
with her a large (and quite noisy) set of keys which she wore on a belt
around her waist. The effect of this was to remind the audience both of
Varia's somewhat marginal status within the family (she is an adopted
daughter) and also of her role in the household – that of housekeeper.
The keys also suggested the need, as far as Varia was concerned, to keep
everything (including her heart?) under lock and key. These properties,
the watch and the keys, become emblems of their owners.

The inventive and *appropriate* use of personal properties in performance
was admired by the actor Ian McKellen in the Channel 4 series, *Playing
Shakespeare*. In discussion with John Barton, he referred to the Peter Hall
production of *Hamlet* to which we have already given some attention.
The actor's eye noted that:

Claudius always had a glass with a drink in it, and because it was tumbler-shaped
I knew that the liquid in it was whisky. That told me something precise about
Claudius: he drinks whisky. It wasn't your all-purpose goblet with nothing in it
but watered-down blackcurrant juice ... In the same production Polonius carried
a briefcase and that was also relevant in a good way. You know what's in a briefcase;

there are papers – to do with law and politics. It wasn't some sort of mocked-up Elizabethan satchel or a scroll which you can't believe has anything written on it.[29]

The invention there derives from the combination of director, and actor. The point is that it *adds* to the meaning of the play in performance and does not detract from it. In your imagined performance text, use of properties must also be guided by this rule.

We find another example of the expressive use of props (this time specified by the dramatist himself) in the scene in Edward Bond's *Saved* that we examined in Chapter One where a baby is stoned to death in a park. The action begins by showing Fred and Len together on an empty stage: Fred is fishing. Although the stage is bare, Bond is careful to specify the properties required in the action. Here, as in Shakespeare, they immediately signify a location and a specific activity. In addition to a fishing-rod, there is a small tin box (on which Len is sitting), a bait-box, an odds-and-ends box, a float-box, a milk bottle, a sugar bottle, a flask and a net. All this paraphernalia is important in helping an audience (and an active reader) understand the significance of both the immediate action, and what occurs in so devastating a manner later in the same scene. Bond uses the props to demonstrate Fred's expertise and mastery of fishing – knowledge which he attempts to impart to Len. The staged action of the hook-baiting is the only time in the whole play when the language employed by a character approaches anything resembling eloquence. The use of the props in the scene helps to define the locale, but more importantly, shows a man in control of at least one aspect of his life. Fred uses tools well, and demonstrates a sense of pride in his skill and knowledge. He is connected to this activity even if alienated from most others:

FRED. Sod!

LEN. Whass up?

FRED. Bait's gone.

LEN. Gone? They've 'ad it away.

FRED. Never.

LEN. Must 'ave.

FRED. More like wriggled off.

LEN. I mounted it 'ow yer said.

FRED. (*winds in.*) Come 'ere. Look.

He takes a worm from the wormbox.

Right, yer take yer worm. Yer roll it in yer 'and t'knock it out. Thass first. Then yer break a bit off. Cop 'old o' that.

LEN. Ta.

FRED. Now yer thread yer 'ook through this bit. Push it up on yer gut. Leave

> it. – Give us that bit. Ta. Yer thread yer other bit on the 'ook, but yer
> leave a fair bit 'angin off like that, why, t'wriggle in the water. Then
> yer push yer top bit down off the gut and camer-flarge yer shank. Got
> it?

LEN.   Thass 'ow I done it.

FRED.   Yeh. Main thing, keep it neat.

He casts. The line hums.

> Lovely.

A long silence.

> The life.

Silence.

How Bond uses properties to define the location in that famous scene
makes a link in dramatic technique between Bond and Shakespeare.
Another theatrical link can also be made by seeing the fishing-gear as
tools in a process skilfully controlled by Fred. This connection is with
Bertolt Brecht. John Willett remarked in *The Theatre of Bertolt Brecht*:

... work itself was given special attention in all Brecht's productions. The jobs
done by his characters, whether plucking a chicken [as in scene two of *Mother
Courage*] ... or scrubbing a man's back in the bath [as Grusha does for the Peasant
in *The Caucasian Chalk Circle*], always had to be done properly, as if they had a
lifetime's practice behind them. They could never be allowed to degenerate into
'business': a botched-up imitation of activities which to Brecht were at once
beautiful and socially important.[30]

In the preface to *Galileo* Brecht stated that he wanted his properties to
be 'realistic'. These realistic properties he then uses with great skill in the
creation of his dramatist's text. If you have read the poem by Brecht at
the beginning of this chapter, you will have seen a dramatist acknowledging not just the importance of properties in making meaning in performance, but also paying tribute to the skilful and inventive choice of personal
properties by the actress Helen Weigel. You too, as active readers, can,
and should, choose appropriate properties and consider what they may
bring to the meaning of the scene or incident in which they are to be used.
For instance in Brecht's *Mother Courage*, much use is made of properties
as tools that people use in order to earn their living. The wagon of Mother
Courage and her children is a property of work that presents to the
audience a visual economic metaphor of Capital literally yoked to Labour
(Eilif and Swiss Cheese are harnessed to it and pull it). A telling use by
Brecht of tools as personal props occurs in two scenes from *Mother
Courage* that we have already considered. In scene three Brecht directs
that Yvette should be seen 'sewing at a coloured hat'. She has her bright-
red boots standing close by. Both the hat and the boots are the essential

tools of her trade (she is a prostitute), used to make her more attractive to her clients and worn as a mark of her profession. When Yvette re-enters the action in scene eight, the hat and the boots are replaced by a stick, upon which her broken body must now lean for support.

When a dramatist specifies the use of a specific property as part of the action (especially if it is a personal prop), he often intends it to work as a visual metaphor and as an active ingredient in the promoting of an appropriate mood or atmosphere. In Shakespeare's *Macbeth*, the lighted taper carried by Lady Macbeth in the sleepwalking scene is obviously functioning in this capacity representing a vulnerable little light of conscience in an otherwise dark and lost soul. The use of the prop does something else. It is important, I feel, that the audience, and perhaps the actress too, should sense that the light could actually be extinguished in performance. The resulting recognition of the risk being taken in performance by the actress which is imparted to the audience, both reflects and intensifies their concern for her plight. In other words, the taper signifies, in this context, a series of connected ideas about the forces of light and darkness at war in this play, and it also can be used theatrically to make the audience *feel* the threat to order (the order being the smooth running of the text-in-performance) that is there because the flame might go out.

The creative use of properties in performance to make atmosphere through establishing a sense of risk is nowhere better illustrated than in Peter Brook's now-legendary production of Shakespeare's *A Midsummer Night's Dream* for the RSC.[31] Brook saw his main theatrical challenge in presenting this play to a seventies audience, as getting them to experience, if not to believe, in the magical world in which the action takes place. He had to find a language, a performance text, that was capable of articulating that magical world. The skilful use of properties formed part of the vocabulary of magic. In Act II, Scene i, Puck is instructed by Oberon to locate a charm:

Fetch me that flower – the herb I show'd thee once.
The juice of it on sleeping eyelids laid
Will make or man or woman madly dote
Upon the next live creature that it sees.

(lines 169–72)

In the performance text, Puck re-entered on a trapeze with the magic charm represented by a silver plate, balanced on the end of a long rod, which he spun rapidly. On seeing him, Oberon, himself swinging on a trapeze but at a lower level, looked up to ask, 'Hast thou the flower there?

Welcome, wanderer.' (line 247). As the fairy king spoke these lines, Puck leant over and flipped the still-spinning plate down through the air to be caught and spun in turn by Oberon: 'Ay, there it is.' (line 248). In the split-second that it took for the plate to fall and be caught, a surge of excitement ran through the theatre audience, touching and uniting them in a shared and 'magical' moment. The trick worked through a combination of imagination and skill on the part of the actors; it worked for the spectators because they knew the feat was not foolproof: the magic could fail, but it didn't.

In the episode that I have just described, the director used his creative imagination to augment Shakespeare's text. What he made in the performance text was a theatre language which enabled the audience to experience the magical world of the play. Their reading of that show opened up the text through a demonstration of skill that aroused admiration and delight, and made concrete and real the distinction between the world of the fairies, and that of the mortals. Brook's use of the property, the spinning plate, served to unlock something imprisoned in the text by late-twentieth-century scepticism and faith in rationality.

Some of the most effective use of props that I have seen was in Terry Hand's production for the RSC of *Richard II*. We have already discussed this play in terms of casting; now I want to look at how properties were used by the director and actors to emphasize the differences between the two men. Alan Howard as the king emphasized Richard's ability to enact the role of monarch: his natural (because inherited by due right and succession) ability to make the most of life's '. . . little scene, To monarchize, be feared, and kill with looks'. Bolingbroke, on the other hand, is shown to be ill-at-ease with the public role of kingship – with affairs of pageantry and state – while more familiar and more capable of commanding political reality. In the deposition scene (Act IV, Scene i) the director emphasized the importance of the direction given prior to Richard's entry: *'Re-enter York, with Richard, and Officers bearing the regalia.'* It is the regalia, orb, sceptre and the crown itself, that are crucial to the playing of this scene in performance. Those properties immediately signalled a very specific meaning to the Elizabethan audience, and perhaps much of their significance is still current today. The crown is, of course, the symbol of kingship. Worn on all public state occasions, it immediately indicates the status of the wearer (our own Queen Elizabeth wears a state crown when, for example, opening Parliament). The sceptre is the symbol of personal sovereignty, and the orb (a sphere with a cross attached), symbolizes the sovereignty of the monarch over the kingdom as a whole. This authority is endorsed by the cross, which symbolizes the divine right to rule. In Hand's production, when Richard divested himself of his office, he gave the regalia into the hands of Bolingbroke, and almost frog-marched him to the throne:

Now, mark me how I will undo myself.
I give this heavy weight from off my head,
And this unwieldy sceptre from my hand,
The pride of kingly sway from out my heart.
With mine own tears I wash away my balm,
With mine own hands I give away my crown.
                    (IV, i, lines 202–7)

As soon as Bolingbroke possessed the symbols that represented his temporal power and spiritual authority, that authority was undermined because it was immediately apparent in Suchet's performance that he did not know what to do with them. The new king appeared uneasy and unfamiliar with the tools he had acquired. Bolingbroke enthroned as Henry IV, with the orb in one hand, the sceptre in the other, and the crown on his head, was in marked contrast to the bravura public performances of Alan Howard's Richard. Everything about the new king spoke of newness, of unease and unfamiliarity. It was as if, now, David Suchet was miscast. Indeed, in the production Bolingbroke/Henry IV never appeared again in the full regalia of state. For the throne was substituted a desk on which the crown was placed, and the gorgeous robes of state were replaced by dark and sombre clothes more suited to this king of business.

Finally, I want to try to illustrate that as an active reader, you have sometimes not only to note the use of a property, but also *to decide* on the nature as well as the function of the prop, and recognize that by doing so you can actually affect the range of meaning comprising the eventual performance text. Consider again the wooing scene in *Richard III* for this demonstrates why the choice of a specific prop nominated in the dialogue (a sharp-pointed sword) needs to be thought about and given form with care. Thus far we have used this episode between Richard and Lady Anne to illustrate the dramatic significance of so-called silent characters. Towards the end of their dialogue, Richard apparently takes an extraordinary risk when he offers Anne,

... this sharp-pointed sword,
Which if thou please to hide in this true breast,
And let the soul forth that adoreth thee,
I lay it naked to the deadly stroke,
And humbly beg the death upon my knee.
                    (I, ii, lines 174–8)

He then proceeds to admit his guilt in the murder of Anne's father-in-law and husband. Why then does she not immediately kill him? In the Olivier film it was obviously supposed to be because she had already fallen under the irresistible charm of this superman. However, for Anne to seize the opportunity for revenge, in the circumstances I have previously outlined (she is observed, young, vulnerable, isolated and a woman), is extremely hard but perhaps not beyond the bounds of possibility. What might in fact (and does in my imaginary performance) prevent her from killing Richard is the sword itself. The only description of the weapon comes from Richard. Although the stage directions indicate that it is a sword belonging to him ('*He lays his breast open. She offers at it with his sword*') there is nothing in the dialogue to suggest that it actually belongs to Richard. If the actor playing him were to move quickly and take a sword from the hands of one of the silent on-stage characters (say from Tressel or Berkeley), then the weapon could justifiably be a heavy two-handed sword. Obviously there is a great deal of difference between offering a young and slight girl a dagger and giving her a sword almost as large as herself. I have seen the former result in Anne's striking at Richard and being restrained by pinning her against the coffin. Encumbering her with a massive and unfamiliar weapon places her in a frustrating and humiliating posture, emphasizing her helplessness in the hands of Richard.

The choice in performance of the property concerned can thus show very different interpretations of the actions. If you decide the sword belongs to Richard himself, his personal weapon, light and, as he says, 'sharp', then you will emphasize in performance the magnitude of both the risk he takes and of his personal charisma in having the confidence and nerve to take it. But if the sword is heavy and cumbersome and belongs not to Richard but to one of the onlookers, a sword perhaps designed either for ceremonial use or for use by a professional soldier, Richard's providing Anne with the weapon is shown as the action of a clever, calculating and totally cynical man. This example shows how a property can be important in making meaning. A change in properties radically alters interpretation and makes it possible to question the traditional audience response of reluctant admiration for Richard's virtuoso performance in seducing Anne. If an audience is made to see that there is no real physical risk involved for Richard, and that the 'victory' is hollow because the combatants were never remotely equal to begin with, then the view of the accomplished seducer must be more difficult to sustain.

Sound Effects

Be not afeared; the isle is full of noises,
Sounds and sweet airs, that give delight, and hurt not.

(The Tempest, III, ii, lines 136–7)

Michael Hattaway reminds us in his very useful and interesting book *Elizabethan Popular Theatre,* that it was probably the wadding from a cannon shot fired for effect during a performance of *Henry VIII* in 1613 that set fire to the thatched roof of the first Globe theatre and resulted in the conflagration that destroyed it. Ben Jonson, a contemporary of Shakespeare, and like him a successful professional playwright, took time in the preface to the 1601 edition of his play *Everyman in his Humour* to satirize the then current fashion for elaborate stage effects brought about by primitive, but effective, stage technology:

He rather prays you will be pleased to see
One such today as other plays should be;
Where neither chorus wafts you o'er the seas,
Nor creaking throne comes down the boys to please;
Nor nimble squib is seen to make afeared
The gentlewoman; nor rolled bullet heard
To say it thunders; nor tempestuous drum
Rumbles to tell you when the storm doth come.[32]

Despite Jonson's objection, the use of the rolled bullet, and other methods for making sound effects, kept the stage hands busy during performances of most Elizabethan and Jacobean plays. The extent of their activity is very well documented in Peter Thompson's chapter, '*Macbeth* from the tiring house', in his study of *Shakespeare's Theatre.*

Hattaway suggests that the hut you can see in the famous De Witt drawing of the Swan Playhouse, perched above the roof that projects out over part of the platform, housed both machinery of the kind objected to by Ben Jonson, and,

In the more lavish playhouses it may have also contained at least one large bell, possibly with a rope that could be pulled from the stage, to serve as an 'alarum' and, in the absence of clocks, to mark the passage of time. Its sounding was heard to great effect at the close of *Doctor Faustus.*[33]

As we have seen, such a bell was also put to effective dramatic use in the opening scene of *Hamlet,* both as a mark of time passing as when Barnardo remarks ''Tis now struck twelve. Get thee to bed, Francisco', (line 7) and also a splendid and atmospheric cue for the first entry of the ghost of Hamlet's father.

BARNARDO: Last night of all,
                When yond same star that's westward from the pole
                Had made his course t' illume that part of heaven
                Where now it burns, Marcellus and myself,
                The bell then beating one –
                Enter the Ghost   (lines 35–9)
MARCELLUS:Peace! break thee off; look, where it comes again!
                                                            (line 40)

Sound effects, like properties, help in the creation of an appropriate mood and atmosphere; they can also be used to inform the audience (and the perceptive reader) of the significance of the action they are witnessing. For example, the creation of the sound of thunder which opens the text of *Macbeth*, signifies to the audience the unrest and disturbance of the natural order the ensuing action is to chronicle. The sound also provides a perfect background to the 'black and midnight hags' and echoes the noise of bloody battle taking place close by. The storm at sea experienced by Othello and Desdemona in *Othello* likewise prefigures in nature the schism that will wreck and finally destroy that marriage. Mad King Lear, in Act III, Scene ii, throws back at the storm an inner tempest that rages in his mind, 'Blow, winds, and crack your cheeks! rage! blow!' (line 1).

The sounds made by trumpets, the alarums so often used by Shakespeare, are present not only to herald the arrival of an important character, but, originally at least, the more sophisticated ear of the Elizabethan audience might have been able to interpret these sounds very specifically. For example:

. . alarums and retreats signal the course of events to an audience attuned to the military significance of each sound.[34]

Contemporary dramatists also make good use of sound effects. In Act II of Pinter's *The Caretaker*, Davies's fear as he gropes about uncertainly in that dark and cluttered room, is suddenly and dramatically turned into sheer terror as, 'the Electrolux starts to hum' (Act II). Only when the lights come on does he, and the audience, realize what the sound was. We noted when looking at Edward Bond's *Saved* how a sound effect (a heavy steel door being slammed shut on Fred at the beginning of scene seven) economically and graphically represents the location of the action (a prison cell). It also works as an aural metaphor suggesting to the audience that their response to what they have witnessed in scene six (the stoning of the baby) is like that of the state: they literally and metaphorically shut it out. Another almost identical sound effect is used by Ibsen in *A Doll's House*: 'The sound of a door being slammed is heard from below.'

That sound comes at the end of the play, emphasizing eloquently the determination and finality of Nora's decision to leave her husband and children, and signalling the end of one life and, perhaps, the beginning of another. In the chapter that dealt with the printed text, I spoke of the significance in dramatic writing of the juxtaposing of scenes and incidents. The ability to control and shape the sequence of the action is one of the most useful tools a dramatist possesses for manufacturing meaning in performance. But not only visual images can be set side-by-side. Sounds too are used in counterpoint to create meaning. For example, in scene four of *Saved*, Mary, Harry, Pam and Len are watching television in a darkened room. As the action progresses, the sound of a baby crying is heard, lasting throughout the duration of the scene. This cry for help is juxtaposed with the volume of the television which Pam deliberately increases to shut out the sound of her child. The two sounds create a terrible crescendo of noise that reverberates inside the heads of the audience. It is, almost literally, unbearable.

In the final minutes of *Hedda Gabler*, Ibsen uses a sound to signal these last moments of Hedda's life. As Mrs Elvsted and Tesman set about reconstructing the manuscript Hedda has destroyed and simultaneously constructing a future that excludes Hedda, they are interrupted by noises from off-stage:

Hedda, off-stage, signals her rising desperation by playing a wild dance tune on the piano

TESMAN: I tell you what, Mrs Elvsted. You shall move into Aunt Julle's and
                 I'll come over in the evenings. And then we can sit and work there.
                 Eh?
MRS ELVSTED: Yes, perhaps that would be the best plan . . .

and her final theatrical and shocking gesture resonates around the theatre: *'a shot . . . heard within'*, as the realization dawns that she has killed herself.

Chekhov is particularly skilled in the creation of mood and atmosphere in his dramas. Watching a good performance of a Chekhov play is to share the experiences and the sensations of the characters before you. Part of this playwright's success in creating mood that can be communicated in performance, is attributable to the use of sound effects. For example, the wonderfully evocative last act of *Three Sisters* uses the following effects:

'The sound of a piano being played off stage.'
The sound of 'a harp and violin somewhere far away.'
'The muffled sound of a distant shot.'

In the closing minutes of the action, the sisters group themselves close together for comfort and mutual support to speak the closing lines against the background of a marching band which is leading the soldiers who have enlivened their community (and leading Vershinin) out of their lives. Another band plays in *The Cherry Orchard*; in fact, throughout the whole of the third act, the sound of the Jewish band can be heard in the background. Its music gives the audience a sense of life and vitality despite the preoccupation of Mrs Ranevsky and Gayev with mourning the passing of the estate. They weep, but the band plays on, just as the life of the play will go on. Indeed their lives too are not over: Paris will, in all probability, be more exciting than the reality, as opposed to the romantic and sentimental idealization that Luviov builds up, of life on a country estate. Gayev will be better off in a bank! The sound of the playing reminds us that Lopakhin, who has bought the cherry orchard, is not a villain, but a liberator.

Perhaps one of the most memorable and well-known uses of sound in Chekhov (and perhaps in any other nineteenth-century dramatist) is that of the breaking string in Act II of *The Cherry Orchard*. You will probably recall that in this act Lopakhin, Trofimov, Varia, Gayev and Liubov Andryeevna are out walking in open country. Their conversation eventually dies away like the setting sun, and Chekhov gives the following famous direction:

They all sit deep in thought; the silence is only broken by the subdued muttering of FEERS. *Suddenly a distant sound is heard, coming as if out of the sky, like the sound of a string snapping, slowly and sadly dying away.*

The sound created in performance has no intrinsic meaning that the audience must search for. It is there not for what it tells us about itself, but for what it reveals about those characters who choose to remark upon it and try to explain it. To Lopakhin, the explanation is simple and straightforward, and reflects this way of looking at life. The sound must have a material cause and can be explained entirely rationally:

... Somewhere a long way off a lift cable in one of the mines must have broken. But it must be somewhere very far away.

Gayev, typically, says anything that will totally contradict Lopakhin. His 'reality' is very far removed from the truth, 'Or perhaps it was some bird ... a heron, perhaps.' Trofimov, the visionary, picks up what Gayev has suggested and extends it. For him the bird is an owl, traditionally a bird of ill-omen. Finally Liubov Andryeevna, the romantic and self-dramatizing heroine, shudders. 'It sounded unpleasant, somehow ...' All

99

except Lopakhin feed off one anothcr, they almost encourage each other in the creation of a drama where, in reality (and only Lopakhin sees the world as it is) there is none.[35]

To sum up: nothing is ephemeral in a performance text. An individual sitting in an audience watching the performance of a play is continually working at making a synthesis of the many and varied signals being transmitted by the actors, the setting, the costumes, thc gestures, lighting, properties, sound effects and so on. You cannot single out any one of these signal generators and give it priority over the rest. An active reader must be aware of the interconnection of everything that is seen and heard in performance.

Preparing for Active Reading

There are some practical things you can do that may help in your discovery of how to animate a printed text and achieve your imaginary performance text.

1. It is useful, and at times necessary, to know how many characters are on stage at any particular moment, and to determine their spatial relationships. If you want to observe the changing shape and thus the pace of the performance, you must be able to monitor the frequency of exits and entrances on to the playing area. The grouping of characters and the organization of scenes can be envisaged more effectively in the mind's eye if you use a simple three-dimensional model: a chess-board serves well to represent the stage. As characters enter or leave, the pieces you have arranged can be moved accordingly (labelling helps make things more clear). Not only does this clarify the staging of the text, it also forces you to make interpretative decisions about the significance of territory, the grouping of characters, and the placing of individual actors within the designated playing space.

2. Try taking two or three editions of any pre-nineteenth-century play and comparing the punctuation by editors of the spoken text. You will find, especially in Shakespeare, a wide discrepancy between the practice of different editors. Punctuation greatly influences meaning. It is therefore worthwhile to explore the effects of removing all editorial punctuation from key speeches and reading the run-on passages for the meanings which emerge. Add your own punctuation after you have read the passage a number of times, being sensitive to the stresses imposed by the rhythm of the language. This can be a surprisingly stimulating exercise, as Peter Hall observed in relation to actors:

When punctuation is just related to the flow of the spoken word, the actor is liberated.[36]

3. Read plays aloud. Of course, when working alone you cannot speak dialogue intended to be enacted in a complex exchange involving several characters, but in soliloquy and duologue you can and will discover a great deal. Reading aloud makes you think about where to place the stress in a line, and what words seem particularly significant or striking. This approach should lead you to consider what individual words *sound* like. Don't worry too much about the quality of your 'performance' – acting

talent isn't needed for the 'thinking aloud' in which you are engaged. A tape-recorder can help to monitor your progress. It is best to start with just one or two lines when beginning to work in this way, and gradually discover the tremendous variety of meanings that you can identify in single lines merely by a change in emphasis or stress. As your confidence grows, you might join in a group-reading. If you do this, remember not to approach the task 'cold': prepare your part in anticipation. Try to look at it as a working actor or actress would: don't come to rehearsal simply to *receive* ideas from the director or the rest of the cast, but *try out* ideas of your own. This can be a valuable way to experiment with an interpretation, and to take imaginative risks.

4. The RSC's principal voice coach, Cicely Berry, teaches that if you have the opportunity to work with a group, it is invariably productive to approach textual study by breaking up long speeches. She recommends splitting them into different parts by giving each member of the group a sentence or a coherent thought that they can then memorize. (It is important to memorize the text so that the group is freed from the need to read from the book.) When each member has learnt his lines it is possible to begin playing games. You can invent whatever activity seems fun, provided it requires both collective and individual verbal communication from the group: that communication can only be achieved through the use of the memorized textual extracts. Get the group to vary as much as possible the way in which words are used. For instance, have them shout whilst the group is still but is spaced as far apart as the dimensions of the room will permit. Then try speaking the lines in a whisper with the group packed tightly together. Don't worry at first about the proper sequence. Eventually try putting the whole speech back together, (remember that this requires knowledge both of individual lines and of those which precede them). In this way, a group can actually do some interesting work on difficult speeches which, left to the individual actor or reader, might prove baffling.

5. Do, of course, go and see as much 'live' theatre as you can, always trying to be aware of the different texts that are together making the performance. As many of you will see the enactment of plays through the medium of television or film, perhaps we should note the following crucial difference between a televized performance and one performed in a theatre before a 'live' audience. That is, in television or film, the camera is always mediating between the audience and the performance text. What you see projected on to the screen has been *selected* by the director and cameraman, whereas, in the theatre, the visual emphasis is made by you. You decide to concentrate on a particular action; upon what gesture appears to have

significance at a particular time in a specific way. In film and television, the close-up or the long-shot, or panning shot, or whatever focus on the action is decided is appropriate, is not in your control. Likewise, in the theatre (unless you get the rare opportunity of being able to move around during the performance) the position from which you watch the text's enactment is fixed. Given the important difference that images on the screen are arranged by a director, and that the arrangement is invariably selective, it is still very useful to be able to have access to filmed or televized versions of plays.

The following check list, while not exhaustive, may prove useful. When I read a play, I try to ask myself how, as a spectator, I would be made aware of the following:

1. *Mood/atmosphere*: How are the mood and atmosphere generated in the perform-ance text?
2. *Location*: Where is the action set and how do we know? Does the location change? If so, when and why and how? Is the action taking place inside or outside? Is it significant either way?
3. *Time*: How is the passing of time signalled to the audience? Does the time of day/time of year change to any great extent during the action? If so, is there any particular significance attached? How are internal time-systems related to each other and reflected in the pace of the play?
4. *Character Identification*: How do we know who is speaking and what his or her relationship is to any listeners? How do we know what we know about them; for example, their class, status, age, occupation?

If you look at the beginning of a play (the exposition), and ask these questions of the printed text, then you will rapidly establish its convention as essentially either representational or non-representational (see Chapter 3 'The Visual Text'). Test your conclusion by comparing a Shakespeare play and one by a later dramatist.

Finally, try to recall the main points we have been examining in our study of the transformation of text into performance. To animate a text you need to bring to your personal study of plays an awareness of the following:

1. *The Shape of a Scene*: How many characters are on stage at any one time? Can you chart the movements on to and off the playing area? How long (approximately) does each scene or section of a scene last in terms of playing time, which, remember, is not the same thing as the time taken to read it on the printed page.
2. *Properties*: What properties are required, and when do you think they are used? Is the choice of a particular kind of prop significant? Can you argue for the choice of a property or invent a need for one which adds to the play's overall meaning?

3. *Costume*: What indication is there in the printed text of what a character wears? Does this change during the action? Can you 'read' the costumes suggested by a dramatist and, if so, what are they saying?

4. *Gesture*: Is there in the printed text, any indication of a particular gesture made by a character – for instance 'Leave wringing of your hands' (Hamlet to his mother Act III, Scene iv, line 35)? Is the action in making social gestures consistent throughout the play? If so, what does this signify and how can you ensure its significance is appreciated?

5. *Silent Characters*: Watch out for actors who may be on-stage in view of the audience but who are given no words to speak. Question their presence and what kind of text it is that they articulate.

This list is not definitive, and I hope that after becoming more acquainted with the process of text-into-performance you will add to it categories of your own. Most importantly, I hope this method of reading will be useful in your work of translating dramatic literature into theatrical events and at the same time will increase your enjoyment of that much-neglected source of reading material: the dramatist's text.

Notes

1. See Janet Suzman, 'Hedda Gabler: the Play in Performance' in *Essays in Celebration of the 150th Anniversary of Henrick Ibsen's Birth*, (ed.) Errol Durbach, London, 1980, p. 97.
2. 'The Caretaker at the Duchess Theatre' in Kenneth Tynan (ed.), *A View of the English Stage*, London, 1975 (new edition 1984), p. 279. This is a fascinating and eloquent collection of essays on English theatrical life from early Olivier performances of Shakespeare to the emergence of the National Theatre.
3. See *Peter Hall's Diaries*, (ed.) John Goodwin, London, 1983, p. 48.
4. *Ibid.*, p. 80.
5. Norman Marshall, *The Producer and the Play*, London 1957, p. 139. Marshall's book is full of hilarious examples of the antics of some nineteenth-century actors and theatre managers in their presentation of the plays of Shakespeare. A less anecdotal, scholarly account of this period and the fashion for elaborate staging is found in Michael R. Booth's *Victorian Spectacular Theatre, 1850–1910*, London, 1981.
6. 'Hedda Gabler: the Play in Performance', p. 83.
7. See *RSC News*, Spring 1985, p. 3.
8. See Stanley Wells's *Royal Shakespeare*, Manchester, 1977, p. 73.
9. Simon Callow, *Being An Actor*, London, 1984, p. 62.
10. *Ibid.*, p. 129. 'Until ideas become translated into sensations, they're of no use whatever to acting.'
11. 'Hedda Gabler: the Play in Performance', p. 85.
12. *Ibid.*, p. 85.
13. *Ibid.*, pp. 93–4.
14. See David Bevington's excellent new study, *Action is Eloquence*, Boston, USA, 1984, p. 136.
15. *Ibid.*, p. 153.
16. A vivid account of this production is given in Stanley Wells's *Royal Shakespeare*.
17. See Timothy O'Brien, 'Designing a Shakespeare Play: Richard II', *Deutsches-Gesellschaft (West) Jahrbuch*, Heidelberg, 1974.
18. Do look as well at Peter Thompson's *Shakespeare's Theatre*, London, 1983. He makes good use of the De Witt evidence in the chapter entitled 'This luxurious circle – the Globe theatre', pp. 36–55.
19. From the prologue to Dekker's *If it be not good the devil is in it* (1612).
20. The very excited reviewer was describing the shipwreck in Madame Vestris's production of *The Chain of Events*, at the Lyceum Theatre, London, in 1852. See *The Producer and the Play*, p. 17.
21. Michael Hattaway, *Elizabethan Popular Theatre*, London, 1982, p. 86.

22. *Ibid.*, p. 87.
23. Stephen Gosson, *Plays Confuted in Five Actions*, London, 1582.
24. *Action is Eloquence*, p. 2.
25. *Bertolt Brecht Poems*, (Eds) John Willett and Ralph Manheim, with the cooperation of Erich Fried, London, 1976.
26. *Peter Hall's Diaries*, p. 189.
27. *Ibid.*, p. 194.
28. *Action is Eloquence*, p. 129.
29. An interesting discussion between Ian McKellen and John Barton is recorded in the former's *Playing Shakespeare*, London, 1984: 'Contemporary Shakespeare', pp. 181–93 (a transcript of the television programmes).
30. *The Theatre of Bertolt Brecht*, London, 1959, p. 159.
31. See an eye-witness account of this production in rehearsal by David Selbourne: *The Making of A Midsummer Night's Dream*, London, 1982.
32. See *Elizabethan Popular Theatre*, p. 31.
33. *Ibid.*, p. 32.
34. *Action is Eloquence*, p. 157.
35. For an interesting and rewarding study of Chekhov's work see J. L. Styan's *Chekhov's Plays in Performance*, Cambridge, 1971.
36. *Peter Hall's Diaries*, p. 180.

Select Bibliography

All quotations from plays by Shakespeare are taken from the New Penguin Shakespeare. Quotations from Ibsen and Chekhov are from the Penguin Classics editions of their work. Brecht's *Mother Courage* is that translated by Eric Bentley and published by Methuen. They are also the publishers of Edward Bond's *Saved* and Harold Pinter's *The Caretaker*.

The following short list of titles indicates work that I have found useful in the preparation of this book.

Barton, John, *Playing Shakespeare*, London, 1984.

Berry, Ralph, *On Directing Shakespeare*, London, 1977.

Bevington, David, *Action in Eloquence*, Boston, USA, 1984.

Brown, John Russell, *Theatre Language: A Study of Arden, Osborne, Pinter and Wesker*, London, 1972. (See Chapter 2 'Harold Pinter: Gesture, Spectacle and Performance', pp. 55–92.)

Callow, Simon, *Being an Actor*, London, 1984.

Gurr, Andrew, *The Shakespearean Stage 1574–1642* (revised edition), Cambridge, 1982.

Hall, Peter, *Peter Hall's Diaries*, (ed.) John Goodwin, London, 1983.

Hattaway, Michael, *Elizabethan Popular Theatre*, London, 1982.

Marshall, Norman, *The Producer and the Play*, London, 1957.

Northam, John, *Ibsen's Dramatic Method*, London, 1953.

Slater, Ann Pasternak, *Shakespeare the Director*, Brighton, 1982. (See in particular her chapters on gestural language, costumes and properties.)

Styan, J. L., *Chekhov's Plays in Performance*, Cambridge, 1971.

Styan, J. L., *Drama, Stage and Audience*, Cambridge, 1975.

Thompson, Peter, *Shakespeare's Theatre*, London, 1983.

Tynan, Kenneth, *A View of the English Stage*, London, 1975 (reissued 1984).

Since the completion of the manuscript of this book, two works have been published that may prove useful and interesting to students of text-into-performance. Both concern the actor's text: Antony Sher has written an account of his preparation for playing Richard III for the RSC in *Year of the King*, London, 1985; and Philip Brockbank has edited a collection of twelve essays by actors on acting Shakespeare – *Players of Shakespeare*, Cambridge, 1985.

PENGUIN PASSNOTES

Carefully tailored to the requirements of the main examination boards (for O-level or CSE exams), Penguin Passnotes are an invaluable companion to your studies.

Covering a wide range of English Literature texts, as well as many other subjects, Penguin Passnotes will include:

ENGLISH LITERATURE

As You Like It
Henry IV, Part I
Julius Caesar
Macbeth
The Merchant of Venice
Romeo and Juliet
Twelfth Night
The Prologue to the Canterbury Tales
Cider With Rosie

Great Expectations
Jane Eyre
A Man For All Seasons
The Mayor of Casterbridge
Pride and Prejudice
Silas Marner
To Kill a Mockingbird
The Woman in White
Wuthering Heights

and OTHER AREAS

Biology
Chemistry
Economics
English Language
French
Geography

Human Biology
Mathematics
Modern Mathematics
Modern World History
Physics

PENGUIN MASTERSTUDIES

Penguin Masterstudies are written by experts to enhance literary appreciation and understanding and are suitable for literary study at advanced level. They are also available in other subjects:

The Penguin Masterstudies will include:

ENGLISH LITERATURE

Hamlet
Measure for Measure
Othello
The Prologue to the Canterbury Tales
The Millers Tale

The Nun's Priest's Tale
Emma and *Persuasion*
Mill on the Floss
Vanity Fair
The Waste Land

and OTHER AREAS

Biology
Chemistry
Geography

Mathematics Vol I Pure
Mathematics Vol II Applied
Physics

PLAYS IN PENGUINS

THE PENGUIN POETRY LIBRARY